The WORLD NEEDS Your F*CKING IDEAS

Benjamin VandenWymelenberg went from being a broke farm boy in Wisconsin to the founder and CEO of a multimillion-dollar business with a social conscience at the heart of its business model.

When he first started, he had no idea how to run a company, no Ivy League business degree for verification of his idea, and no money, but he made it work anyway. He took that first step and learned valuable lessons throughout his journey.

The World Needs Your F*cking Ideas

How to Start a Business That Will Save Our Universe

BENJAMIN VANDEN WYMELENBERG

RUPA

Published by
Rupa Publications India Pvt. Ltd 2023
7/16, Ansari Road, Daryaganj
New Delhi 110002

Sales Centres:
Prayagraj Bengaluru Chennai
Hyderabad Jaipur Kathmandu
Kolkata Mumbai

Copyright © Benjamin VandenWymelenberg

Original English language edition published in 2019 by Buy One. Plant One. Publishing, 2305 Meeting Place, Wayzata Minnesota 55391, USA. Arranged via Licensor's Agent: DropCap Inc.

The views and opinions expressed in this book are the author's own and the facts are as reported by him which have been verified to the extent possible, and the publishers are not in any way liable for the same.

All rights reserved.
No part of this publication may be reproduced, transmitted, or stored in a retrieval system, in any form or by any means, electronic, mechanical, photocopying,
recording or otherwise, without the prior permission of the publisher.

P-ISBN: 978-93-5702-232-3
E-ISBN: 978-93-5702-238-5

First impression 2023

10 9 8 7 6 5 4 2 3 1

Printed in India

This book is sold subject to the condition that it shall not, by way of trade or otherwise, be lent, resold, hired out, or otherwise circulated, without the publisher's prior consent, in any form of binding or cover other than that in which it is published.

This book is for all the humans of Mother Earth who have a great idea that can positively impact the planet. My hope is that reading this book helps you to break down any mental barriers that exist in your own mind and allows you to take the first step (or continue) with your idea.

Within every one of you exists an idea to change the world. Don't let it go to the fucking grave with you. Get out, get up, and do it!

CONTENTS

    ACKNOWLEDGMENTS 9
    DISCLAIMER 11
    INTRODUCTION: JUST A BROKE-ASS FARM BOY 13

1. QUIT THINKING, START DOING, AND COMMIT TO YOUR IDEA 23
2. TURNING FAILURE INTO OPPORTUNITY 37
3. THE GRADUATING MINDSET 45
4. ASK A LOT OF QUESTIONS 55
5. BECOMING A POWERHOUSE THROUGH NETWORKING 67
6. SOMETIMES YOU HAVE TO BE AN ASSHOLE 81
7. GOOD FRIENDS GET YOU OUT OF JAIL; BEST FRIENDS ARE IN THE CELL WITH YOU 95
8. THE COLLECTIVE IS BETTER THAN THE INDIVIDUAL 109
9. DISCONNECT TO RECONNECT 131
10. I HOPE YOU LIKE YOURSELF 143
11. GREAT LEADERS KNOW WHEN TO LEAD AND WHEN TO EMPOWER 157

    CONCLUSION: NOW GO DO IT! 167
    ABOUT THE AUTHOR 171
    APPENDIX I: THE SPARKNOTES VERSION 173
    APPENDIX II: REFERENCE MATERIALS 177

ACKNOWLEDGMENTS

I am eternally grateful to my parents, Peter and Mary Jo VandenWymelenberg, for teaching me everything I needed to know about being a good person and giving back to humanity.

Also, thank you to my wrestling coaches, Matt and Bill Verbeten, for teaching me that my mind and work ethic could be pushed 10X past the competition at a very young age.

And a very special thanks to John Cunningham and David Washburn, the two architectural mentors/bosses I had many years ago. When I approached them with my question about attending graduate school or starting a business, they both wisely advised me—without hesitation—to start my own business, saying that I would learn more in two years of running a business than in any amount of time in a master's program. Without that advice, I wouldn't be where I am today and neither would the tens of millions of trees I've planted in the world.

DISCLAIMER

What you're about to read is a raw and authentic account of my true-life journey as an entrepreneur and an inhabitant of the planet Earth. Some of the names and places have been changed to protect the innocent and the not so innocent. After all, some people are just assholes.

This book is full of crazy stories and uses a lot of F-bombs and other potentially crude language. Despite that straight-up, unfiltered approach, I hope it serves as inspiration to get you to take your best idea to the next level and start a universe-saving business.

Introduction

JUST A BROKE-ASS FARM BOY

Life can be much broader when you realize one simple fact: Everything around you that you call life was made up by people that were no smarter than you and you can change it, you can influence it, you can build your own things that other people can use. Once you have learned that, you will never be the same.

—STEVE JOBS (AMERICAN BUSINESS MAGNATE AND INVESTOR)

Whether you know it or not, the fate of the world rests in your hands.

Climate change, global health crises, and many other social, political, and environmental issues continue to threaten our quality of life and the inhabitability of our planet. The good news, however, is that after reading this book, you're going to save the universe!

Wondering how you're going to rescue humanity from its current collision course with catastrophe? It's simple; all we need are your ideas.

That's right; the world needs your f*cking ideas. They've probably been buried deep in your subconscious, wary of judgment from your peers and fearful of failure for many years. However, humanity needs you to rise to the occasion now more than ever.

I'm certain we all have the ability to change the world, because I see it wherever I go. So many people have amazing ideas to start impact-capable businesses, but something stops them from putting those thoughts into action.

As a serial entrepreneur, I've visited all seven continents and talked to many different people from all walks of life. During those conversations, I've heard incredibly innovative ideas for almost every industry, from farming processes and water purification techniques to technological advances and everything in between. I don't care if your idea is as seemingly insignificant as building a better badminton racket. If playing better badminton helps people to live fuller and happier lives, then save the world from playing shitty badminton and make it happen!

After hearing about so many potentially amazing solutions to the growing list of worldwide problems over the years, I started thinking about why so few of them ever see the light of day. I came to the conclusion that one or more of three misguided concerns is almost always the root cause of such inactivity.

1. People think they need a business degree or background.

No degree? No problem. I was an architectural student with no idea of how to start or run a business. For most of my life, I had no intention of becoming an entrepreneur. Until my senior year in college, my career ambitions were to design sustainable homes with the best available technology in the beautiful state of Colorado.

2. People think they need money or investors.

I was a broke-ass farm boy when I started my business. The best resource I had going for me was an undeniably strong work ethic handed down by two of the hardest-working people I've ever known—my parents. From a young age, I learned to work hard for everything I wanted, which is why I had three jobs to put myself through college. If you can outwork everybody, like I did, money will never be an obstacle.

3. People don't know where to start.

This is likely a combination of procrastination and fear of failure. Do you want to live the rest of your life wondering, "What if I had started a business with my idea?" Regret is a horrible thing to live with and it's even worse to die with. So, it's time to get off your ass, stop worrying about what other people think, and just do it!

Despite popular opinion, failure *is* an option. Who cares if you fail? In that case, at least you can live the rest of your life knowing you did everything you could to make your idea work. Also, understand that there's no limit to the number of attempts you get at starting a business. My first attempt was a failure, but that didn't stop me. In reality, you can fail as often as it takes to get your idea off the ground. You can also start a business from anyplace and with practically nothing, just like I did.

My initial product launch was handmade wooden phone cases in the consumer electronics accessories market, which, in hindsight, wasn't a good choice. It turned out to be one of the worst markets I could have possibly attempted accessing, especially in the United States. At the time, I didn't understand that most electronics accessories were made in China for about ten cents apiece, then sold at the big-box electronics stores for a huge markup. It was almost impossible to compete in that space, especially if you wanted to keep jobs in the United States by making the product domestically, which

I did. As a result, I failed miserably with my initial product launch.

Strangely enough, I'm eternally grateful for that experience. If I had carefully analyzed all the data and waited for the perfect time to unleash my idea on the world, the chain of events that ultimately led to my success would have probably never happened. My entrepreneurial journey would have traveled a much different path, littered with hesitation, procrastination, and far less impact. My early experience is proof positive that sometimes you have to follow your instincts more than anything else, even if they lead you astray.

With that mistake under my belt, I worked on new ideas and never looked back.

Today, I'm the founder and CEO of WOODCHUCK USA, a technology-driven multimillion-dollar manufacturer of customized wood products. By putting my idea into action, hundreds of people are employed around the world today with good-paying full-time jobs. Our motto, "BUY ONE. PLANT ONE.®" is a cause near and dear to my heart, and it has served as the inspiration behind the planting of millions of trees on six continents and a positive global impact on all seven. What started as a seemingly small and relatively insignificant idea—to build wooden iPhone cases—has truly changed the world.

You may think that your ideas are too tiny to have an impact, but based on my own experience, I guarantee that's not the case. If you follow even a handful of the principles detailed in this book, you'll discover how your idea can change the world as well.

Ask yourself, "What kind of world would we live in if *everybody* put their best ideas into action?" I guarantee that the sum of the parts would be much greater than the individual pieces. If everybody was out innovating and taking risks with new ideas, we could make this planet a pretty fucking awesome place to live. We could save entire rain forests, discover new cancer-killing drugs, solve world hunger, and maybe even play better badminton, among other things. The potential of the human spirit is vast and powerful, but you have to take that first step.

Starting and running a business isn't easy, but if a broke-ass farm boy from Wisconsin with no money and no business background can do it, so can you. I had the idea to turn a piece of wood strapped to cardboard with plastic wrap into a prototype for an iPhone case. It was a simple idea that launched a multimillion-dollar company with a global social conscience.

I also never thought I'd write a book. If you'd asked the friends I grew up with whether I'd someday be a book author, they'd have probably said, "Ben? Are you kidding me? He barely even *reads* books and is probably the worst speller I've ever met. He also drops way too many F-bombs."

Now, I'm happy to surprise them. It further illustrates my point that we're all capable of doing things that we mistakenly believe are beyond our abilities. I've never believed in limitations. Fuck limitations! You might not think you're capable of starting a world-changing business, but the truth is that you are.

This is not your boilerplate business book. It's not another step-by-step guide to blah, blah, blah. Instead, you'll find plenty of valuable lessons about the importance of passion, purpose, loyalty, and empowerment. These are the intangibles that have been the keys to my success, and they can be the keys to yours as well.

I'll also take you with me to some of the amazing places I've been. I'm only twenty-eight, but I've already been to some of the most breathtaking places our planet has to offer. For example, I've traveled the sun-soaked desert sands of Saudi Arabia, stood below remote waterfalls in Bali, and witnessed the majestic presence of some of the most magnificent glaciers in Antarctica.

One of the most influential waterfalls of all time, middle of nowhere, Bali

You'll also read about some crazy situations that have crossed my path along the way. I've been sued many times, which is awesome! That might sound strange, but I'll explain it later. I almost got my hand cut off over a traffic dispute in Madagascar, and I've absolutely cheated death a few times.

In chapter 1, you'll read about one of the most important lessons I've learned in business and in life, which is commitment. If I hadn't committed while dirt-biking with my friend at Gorman Canyon in California, not only would there be no WOODCHUCK USA, hundreds of fewer jobs, and millions of fewer trees in the world, but I would be dead.

Fortunately, I made that commitment and now I'm here to tell you about it, along with this important piece of advice: the world needs your fucking ideas!

Chapter One

QUIT THINKING, START DOING, AND COMMIT TO YOUR IDEA

———

The only impossible journey is the one you never begin.
—TONY ROBBINS (AMERICAN MOTIVATIONAL SPEAKER AND AUTHOR)

What happens if you have a game-changing idea to build something great but never take action on it?

Absolutely nothing.

You will go to your grave holding on to an idea that could have positively impacted humanity, but instead it will remain in your decaying brain, serving as nothing more than worm food for years to come.

Always remember that nothing in business or life is perfect. You can engineer a product to death, apply for patents that take years to finalize, and research the shit out of everything, but nothing will happen if you don't quit thinking and get started.

Striving for perfection may sound like a noble and worthy cause for aspiring entrepreneurs, but obsessing over an idea and never turning it into reality makes you something quite different: a *wantrepreneur*. I was never a wantrepreneur, but my idea did take a while to manifest.

FRANKEN-CASES FOR BEER MONEY

In college, I worked three jobs to pay for my education. One of them was in the studio of an architectural company called Cunningham Group, where I used a laser cutter to stick wooden models together. That gig was a great fit because it was the only job I could find that would let me show up after cheer practice and get paid to work until three in the morning.

One day before work, I took a header while Rollerblading and shattered my iPhone. Luckily for me, the device still worked, but the screen was shattered, so I had to endure shoving shards of glass into my face every time I used the phone, which gave me an idea when I got to work that night. As I was cutting some wood veneers in the studio,

I thought, "I should totally cut one of these things to fit the back of my phone."

Inspiration turned into motivation and I quickly went to work, cutting out a backing for the phone made from a piece of mahogany—real wood veneer—and wrapping it in plastic wrap. This protected the device from further damage and prevented the broken glass from stabbing me in the face, which resulted in unnecessary bleeding. Honestly, it looked like the worst third-grade art project you've ever seen. It was a total Frankenstein of smartphone cases. But strangely enough, people thought it looked pretty cool.

When I brought my Franken-case-looking iPhone protector to cheer practice the next day, a couple of my buddies saw it and said, "Dude, that thing is awesome! Can we buy one from you? We'll give you twenty bucks," which happened to be just enough for a case of beer.

I thought to myself, "It cost me about a penny to make the damned thing, so I'd be an idiot to not do it. After all, beer money is still better than no money, especially to a starving college student."

You're probably thinking, "So that's when you had your aha moment? That's when it all came together: your idea for a multimillion-dollar business? All of a sudden, you went from a beer-drinking architecture student to a visionary entrepreneur, right?"

Not exactly. In fact, I made about fifteen of those Frankencases for friends without any thought of taking the idea further. An interesting side note is that I still have one of those original cases.

Frankencase #1: The First Woodchuck Case" (Plastic wrap implementation at its finest)

KNOW YOUR *WHY*

My makeshift device finally turned into a clear vision of something much bigger and more impactful about four to five months later, when my buddy Kevin and I watched a TED Talk hosted by the legendary motivational speaker Simon Sinek.

Kevin Groenjes was and still is the best friend I've ever had. We were introduced by a mutual friend about a year before I made my first Franken-case for beer money. Instantly, we hit it off and have been close ever since.

About two-and-a-half months after making the commitment to start my business, I asked Kevin to be my right-hand man because we always had a contagious energy together, which was incredibly valuable because I needed someone to match my determination to build the foundation of my business. I knew that Kevin and I would go into beast mode together, work all hours of the night, and hit the ground running.

We watched that TED Talk from the living room couch of my rental house in the ghetto of South Minneapolis. The couch was one of those old beat-up pieces of furniture you might find curbside with a big "FREE" sign on it. Nonetheless, it was incredibly comfortable, and it served quite admirably as the centerpiece to our office/living room for the first six months or so of the business.

Neither Kevin nor I knew anything at all about business, but we plugged my laptop into the television one night and watched Sinek's incredibly impactful and motivating TED Talk. He said that people don't buy *what* you do; they buy *why* you do it. He tells business leaders and entrepreneurs to start by asking themselves *why* they want to start a business or *why* they're in business.

Sinek's point is that it's not enough to just want to make a bunch of money. There's going to be a lot of turbulence in starting and running a business, and the sheer motivation of earning more money won't be enough to get you through that. He suggests that the key to surviving the volatile highs and lows of being a business owner is knowing your *why*.

That concept made a lot of sense to Kevin and me, and it absolutely blew our minds. It inspired a conversation almost immediately because we shared some common interests, like environmentalism and job creation. Not long after watching that TED Talk and talking about Sinek's revelation, we came up with our *why*: we wanted to bring nature back into people's lives, create jobs in the US, and build high-quality American products.

Notice our *why* didn't include anything about how much money we wanted to make or specifically mention wooden smartphone cases.

Making money doing anything is nice because you need money to live, but if Kevin and I were in business exclusively to make money, we could have been architects, personal trainers, writers, or anything else. Kevin was a kinesiology major and could have earned a nice living as a therapist or personal trainer. I was an architecture major and could have made plenty of money designing and constructing buildings.

Did we have any special affinity for smartphone cases? Nope. Does anybody? However, we were deeply passionate about our *why*. Nature, jobs, and the satisfaction of creating a high-quality product were all sentiments we could get fired up about. That was what really mattered. When we unwrapped those common motivational factors, we didn't need to wait any longer. We were ready to quit thinking, start doing, and commit to our idea.

Key Takeaway #1: You can make money doing almost anything in life, but by knowing your why, *you can make money, feel fulfilled, and create significant positive impact for yourself and everyone around you.*

ON AND OFF TARGET

Maybe six months after watching that powerful TED Talk, Kevin and I approached Target and Best Buy with our *why*. We didn't just brazenly walk in there and announce,

"Hey everybody, look at our kick-ass wooden smartphone cases! Aren't they awesome? How many do you want to buy today?"

Our pitch went a little more like, "Look, we're incredibly passionate about what we want to do. We want to bring nature back into people's lives, create jobs in the US, and build high-quality American products, and we would love to partner with you to make those things happen."

That interaction eventually led to us selling our wooden cases for the iPad in all eighteen hundred Target stores and select Best Buy locations. Unfortunately, we didn't perform any due diligence in reading the fine print of the deals we signed. If we had, we would have realized that the deals were based on consignment, which made it a terrible idea. Consignment meant that if the products didn't sell (and they didn't), we had to take them all back and not get paid for a penny of them.

The end result was that we were paid a small sum of money up front, but received nothing for the products that didn't sell, which was almost all of them. The bigger problem was that we had already spent all of our friends' and families' money on high-end packaging to complement the high-end product, which was a fine idea. But when that product didn't sell, it meant we had no money to pay anyone back. All things considered, we were about $500,000 in debt.

If our *why* had only been concerned with making money, we would have slammed on the brakes of this operation and closed the doors at that moment. However, we still believed strongly in our *why* and we'd learned some things as well. One of those lessons was that selling these wooden smartphone cases to retail establishments was not the way to make it happen.

The bottom line is that we were still committed to our idea, and that's a big lesson I've learned in life and business. You have to commit, because indecision could have disastrous consequences. Take, for example, the time I went dirt-biking with a friend at Gorman Canyon in Northern California.

COMMIT OR DIE

I'm a huge fan of motorcycles, so when a friend from one of my entrepreneurial groups, named Ian, asked me to go dirt-biking at Gorman Canyon, I jumped at the chance. Gorman Canyon is a beautiful, natural landscape of mountainous terrain in Northern California. I figured it would be an intense experience to go dirt-biking there, and I have never been more right about anything.

I was pretty sure I'd be able to keep up, so off we went. The weather was perfect when we got there, and we enjoyed the views of some of the most picturesque areas we had ever seen. After we had ridden around for a while, Ian stopped and said, "See that mountain ahead? We're going to ride up that motherfucker later."

Point-blank, I said, "Ian, there's no way in hell I'm riding up that beast. Fuck that!"

Initially, Ian didn't completely acknowledge my resistance and kept riding toward the mountain. It took a while to get there, but the more we rode around, the more comfortable I got. I hadn't done any serious dirt-biking in a few years, so I was a little rusty when we first started. But by the time we got to the base of the mountain, I was feeling pretty good about my dirt-biking ability again, so I said, "Alright, I'm ready. Let's do it."

"Awesome, dude. You're going to love it! Just one thing, though," Ian said in a disturbingly nonchalant manner. "There's one crazy turn up there. If you don't commit to pushing hard down into that turn, you will fall off a fucking cliff and die...got it?"

I stared at him blankly for a few seconds, not knowing how to respond. He finished his weirdly motivational speech by ignoring the dumbfounded expression on my face and matter-of-factly saying, "Cool, let's go!" Then he rode away, completely expecting me to follow.

After about fifteen to twenty seconds of pausing to fully understand what I was about to do, I decided it was now or never and hit the gas to catch up to my friend.

When we began to climb the mountain, Ian accelerated about twenty yards ahead of me. A few minutes later, his bike seemed to completely vanish from the path ahead, leaving nothing but a small trail of dust behind him.

As I rode on for another twenty-five yards or so, a wicked ninety-degree turn appeared from out of nowhere, and immediately in front of me was a few-thousand-foot drop. This was no hill I would have tumbled down and gotten a few bumps and bruises from, or maybe a broken arm or leg. This was the kind of drop where my body would have likely disintegrated upon impact, sort of like Wile E. Coyote in those old Road Runner cartoons, when he slips on a banana peel, slides off a cliff, and all you see is a tiny cloud of dust kick up from below. (Beep! Beep!)

Fortunately, I kept hearing Ian's voice echoing in my brain: "Commit, commit, commit!" In an instant, I closed my eyes and leaned right into the turn as hard as I could. At the same time, Ian's voice was replaced with my own: "Ben, you fucking idiot; you're going to die now!"

When I initially opened my eyes, I wasn't sure if I was dead, free-falling ten thousand feet and about to be dead, or in a dream where I was about to be greeted by the Scarecrow, the Tin Man, and the Cowardly Lion. Another two to three hundred yards down the trail, I finally realized, "Holy shit! I did it! I'm alive!"

Ian and I rode for another half mile or so before we stopped to collect ourselves. I said, "I can't believe we fucking did that. I thought I was going to die for sure."

"I knew you would do what you had to, but what did you learn from that?" Ian asked me.

I told him, "I learned to fucking commit; it's the only option."

What an experience that was! It was one of those occasions that you can't truly fathom unless you've actually experienced it for yourself. However, I want to take this opportunity to express to you how valuable that lesson regarding commitment has been to me. It has played out numerous times in my life since then. I'm incredibly grateful for that experience at Gorman Canyon now because, from that point on, I only go into something with all of my energy or not at all. For me, it's everything or nothing; all-in or all-out; commit or die.

Key Takeaway #2: Whether you're involved in personal, business, or financial relationships, you need to commit. You can't half-ass anything and expect positive results...ever. You need to give 110 percent or nothing.

Dirt-biking Gorman Canyon, California (This could have been the last picture taken of me if I didn't commit.)

Chapter Two

TURNING FAILURE INTO OPPORTUNITY

Success is not final, failure is not fatal: it is the courage to continue that counts.

—WINSTON CHURCHILL (PRIME MINISTER OF THE UNITED KINGDOM, 1940–1945 AND 1951–1955)

If that original deal with Target and Best Buy had worked out, we would have never accepted the next deal, which turned into a long-lasting business relationship that WOODCHUCK is still part of today.

Just as Kevin and I were wondering what to do with the nearly sixty thousand iPad cases we had to take back from the big-box stores, a guy named Matt (who later became a great friend of mine) from Red Bull called us and asked, "Hey, I'm calling about the wooden smartphone cases you guys make. Can you etch logos and put names on those things? I want to give them to seventeen athletes we work with. I'll pay full price, but I need them in California by tomorrow. Can you do it?"

To this day, I have no idea where Matt saw us with our product, but at that time we were desperate to unload even two of those things, so I said, "Fuck yeah, we can do that." I would have jumped in the car right away and driven them there myself if I had to.

Seventeen products sold wasn't going to do much for our $500,000 debt, but a new business channel definitely could, and that's what we spotted. We wondered if other people would pay to custom-brand our products as well. If they paid full price, we figured that's a hell of a lot better than Target giving us 30 percent for selling them in their stores. Also, we wouldn't have to worry about getting them shipped back to us for any reason. It seemed like we were onto something big.

We showed up at the North American Red Bull HQ office the next day with seventeen customized wooden smartphone cases. When Matt received them, he said, "Guys, these things are fucking awesome! Our athletes are going to love having their names etched into the cases. Great job!"

Then he took the conversation a little further. He said,

"You know what? I'm a marketing guy and everything is last-minute for me. I have an event next week, and if you guys want to get more of these things to me, I'll buy them. Actually, I've always got an event or two going on where I can use something like this, and we can probably hook up for a bunch of stuff. What do you think?"

At the time, Kevin and I were so poor that we were splitting the same sandwich for lunch on most days, so we were somewhat preoccupied with eating all the free food we could in Matt's office while he was talking. But once we heard the words *buy more*, we stopped stuffing our faces and started listening. "Yes sir! We can do that," we said with our mouths full of cheese and crackers.

Our dedication to our *why* had paid off in a big way. If we had been only focused on the money aspect of the business, we could have easily told Matt, "It's seventeen cases, dude. We have sixty thousand of these things ready to be burned in a landfill somewhere. Thanks, but no thanks." But we didn't. We still had our motivation of bringing nature back into people's lives, creating jobs, and building quality American products.

As small as that initial order was, we jumped at the opportunity, and today Red Bull is a multimillion dollar per year partner of ours. The deal has around 200 percent greater margins than we would have made in any retail partnership. Good thing we didn't thumb our noses at seventeen cases being too small potatoes for us.

FINDING OFFICE SPACE

As it turns out, another opportunity was born from what could have mistakenly been perceived as nothing more than failure with the big-box stores.

While we were getting WOODCHUCK off the ground and creating other opportunities similar to our relationship with Red Bull, we recognized that we had a need for actual office space. Until this point, we had mostly been squatting in other people's work areas. Obviously, that's not a viable long-term solution.

Our initial search for a place to call home opened our eyes to a big problem for startups and entrepreneurs everywhere. Most property owners who rented office space asked for two to three months of rent up front and demanded to see two years of financials to prove profitability. We thought, "What the fuck? Most startups haven't even been in business for a year, let alone have two years of profitability under their belt. How the shit does anybody secure decent office space?"

Once again, we were committed to our *why*. Instead of hanging our heads, kicking at the dirt, and giving up, we interpreted the challenge as more of an opportunity to do something positive.

We knew that there were hundreds of other businesses in the same position we were in who needed space. They also had no money and hadn't been established long enough to show two years of financials. I thought if I could partner with someone to build a coworking space, I could rent it out to some of the more innovative and creative startups in the area. This would not only make some good money for us, but it would also serve the larger entrepreneurial community with a big-time solution to a serious need.

After some bumps in the road, I pitched my idea of coworking space to a couple of business partners of mine. I told them, "I have around twenty or thirty startups that need space right away, but they can't afford the crazy cost of renting a big office building. Obviously, I don't have the money to buy a building myself, but if you become partners in this venture, I'm sure I can get them on board."

They responded, "There's a building for sale down the street that's about seventy thousand square feet. If we buy it and renovate it, can you take care of all the design work and architecture, and rent it out? We don't want to pay a real estate agent, either."

"Done, done, and done," I told them.

We became partners in a coworking-space venture and had the building 100 percent filled within three months. The icing on the cake was that we received around three times the rent that we had initially estimated.

That building has since turned into a bigger complex that we're developing into a 200,000 square-foot facility that we expect to fill to capacity as well. When we're done, over one thousand employees will have the office space they need to innovate and create the next great product or service. For me, that's the best part of the business. I get to evaluate all these startups and businesses with great ideas, business models, and plans to change the world. In that way, I get to play a role in their success, and that's a hugely satisfying feeling for me.

Now, you tell me: How does that initial big-box situation with a $500,000 debt look now? Does it look like the end of the road? Does it look like total failure? Or does it look more like opportunity? Stay the course with your business as long as you're aligned with your *why*, because you never know what might happen next.

Key Takeaway #3: Opportunities are often hidden; you may need to look really fucking hard to find them. When you do, and you're able to view challenges or hardship as an opportunity, the rewards will be tremendous.

What are you going to do when life or business hits you in the face with a hard right hook? Are you going to stay down on the ground, huddled in the fetal position, letting passersby take turns at kicking you to the curb? Or are you going to get up, no matter how much pain you're in, and turn things around?

There's no benefit to doing nothing at all. This is the only life you get, so you'd better make the most of it. When life punches you in the face, you may as well put some ice on it and move forward. The world needs you to.

Chapter Three

THE GRADUATING MINDSET

Being sued by your own record company; that's even better than winning a Grammy.

—NEIL YOUNG (GRAMMY WINNER/
PROUD LAWSUIT RECIPIENT)

Before we found a more permanent solution to our need for an office, we rented space from a big printing company in Minnesota. The owner of the company was a highly successful businessperson named Trish, who discovered our company through a mutual friend.

TWISTED SISTER

One day, Trish asked to meet with Kevin and me because she said she loved our energy and what we were trying to do for the environment. She invited us into her office and told us, "Hey guys, I know how hard it is to get started. At this point in my career, I'd like to help other people with great ideas to make it in the business world. So, here's what I'm going to do. Why don't you move into my printing office? You can set up shop in there until you start making money. In the meantime, I'll help you guys navigate the industry, and we'll see if we can make a big impact together."

Trish didn't make us sign any contracts, which made it seem like we would have been fools to not accept her offer. Shortly after that, we ended up becoming very close. In fact, I thought of her as a sister and mentor at one point. When times got tough, I knew I could call her and get some good advice about business or life.

After a while, Trish handed us an American Express card and said, "Take this; it's unlimited. Hit the streets and do some serious marketing with it. Rent some billboards, get a nice condo to stay in, and get your products in the stores. Go high-end, too. Don't cheap out on anything, because you need to keep up a high-end image."

"Sure. Here's the thing," I said. "We don't have any money to pay you back."

Trish looked at us somewhat incredulously and said, "No,

no, no. I'll cover it. We'll worry about that stuff later. Just go work your asses off for now and focus on blowing up this brand."

Not long after that, Kevin and I were driving around California in luxury sports cars, renting an outrageous condo in Santa Monica, and spending crazy money on marketing. I remember thinking at the time, "Shit. Is this a normal lifestyle for a businessperson? It seems a little too good to be true." Not long after posing that question, I got my answer, which was categorically, no, that was not normal, and yes, it was definitely too good to be true.

A couple of months after our spending spree, Trish asked to meet with me for lunch. This time, she didn't look quite as helpful or nearly as sisterly. "Hey Ben," she said, "I need you to start paying me back for all that stuff I helped you with."

PAYBACK REALLY IS A BITCH

After three to four seconds of an incredibly awkward silence, I came out with, "Wait a second. Did you say something about paying you back?"

With total seriousness and not a hint of friendliness, she responded, "Yeah, you know, for all those billboards and things you bought." She elaborated, "Look, I need a couple million dollars from you guys."

I said, "Trish, we have zero dollars, so..."

"Too bad," she said. "You owe me a lot of money, and if I don't get it soon, you'll be hearing from my lawyers."

I left her office that day not knowing what the hell we were going to do next. All of a sudden, the person who had been our biggest supporter turned on us. About three weeks later, she locked us out of the space we were using at her printing office. In fact, she hired a security guard, armed with a loaded handgun, to stand in front of the building with specific instructions to keep Kevin and me out. Of course, that wouldn't have been so bad except... all of our equipment was still in there. Worst of all was the $1.5 million lawsuit we received just a couple weeks later.

CONGRATULATIONS, YOU'VE BEEN SUED!

As a kid, I remember thinking that anybody who got sued was a thief and a terrible person. They usually went to jail, I thought. Or maybe they were put to death by lethal injection. Okay, maybe not death, but I definitely thought people's lives were ruined once they got sued.

I didn't know where to turn at that point, and I was in

a severely depressed mindset. Once again, however, I stayed true to my *why*. I wasn't going to give up, so I called my mentor, Ken Rutkowski, who is still my mentor today. If anybody could help me, it was Ken.

My conversation with Ken was so memorable that I remember exactly where I was standing at the time we spoke. It was in front of a liquor store in the ghetto near Hermosa Beach. My head was leaning against a rusty signpost, and I kept thinking about how completely fucked I was.

When he picked up the phone, I said, "Ken, I am absolutely fucked! I'm getting sued for $1.5 million. I won't be able to pay that in a hundred lifetimes."

"Ben, are you serious?" Ken asked.

"Yeah, totally fucking serious."

"Well then, congratulations!" he said.

At that point, I started to wonder if Ken was high on some kind of weird brain-altering substance or had just come back from Burning Man. Neither of those things was true, of course. Ken is too smart for anything like that. I asked him, "Ken, can you hear me okay? Because I just told you I'm getting sued for $1.5 million and you wished me congratu-fucking-lations!"

"Ben, yes...congratulations! I can hear you fine, and that's great news because it means you've made it! You've leveled up," he said. "Don't you realize that most billionaires have about fifteen different lawsuits going on at the same time? If you don't get sued at some point, you're not trying hard enough."

I thought about what he was trying to tell me, and said, "You know what? I think that actually makes a lot of sense."

Exactly at that moment, my shift in mindset occurred. Total financial disaster had instantly transformed into my official arrival on the entrepreneurial scene. I was getting sued for the first time, which wasn't the end of the world. It was actually awesome!

Almost any situation is entirely about mindset. You can view setbacks—like million-dollar lawsuits—as certain death, or you can look at them as opportunity. There is a silver lining to any situation, but you might have to look really hard to find it sometimes. If you have a kick-ass mentor like Ken in your corner, that's probably a pretty good place to start looking.

Ken educated me to always look for that silver lining, but, more importantly, he made me realize that I still had a lot to learn. One of those lessons was that we can experience the most personal growth in times of our greatest emotional pain and turmoil. This speaks to something I call the "graduating mindset."

Every time you experience a painful situation in life or business, you have an opportunity to graduate your mindset. In life, if you're presented with a relationship issue that challenges you, that's an opportunity to enhance your tolerance for emotional pain, which will lead to a greater ability to experience love.

The same is true in the business world. That pending lawsuit made me grow exponentially as a person and an entrepreneur. I learned how to deal with the pain of feeling like I was at rock bottom. My dreams of changing the world seemed like they had come to an end, until Ken changed my perspective.

Key Takeaway #4: Rather than getting discouraged about a particularly difficult challenge in life or in business, you should train your brain to "graduate" your current mindset and elevate to its future state. Ask yourself, "How would my future self wish I was thinking about this specific situation?" Or call a mentor and ask them, "How would you think about this specific situation?"

There will be a million opportunities for you to "graduate your mindset" throughout the execution of your idea. The better you get at doing that, the more successful you'll be. A prime example of this is the life story of my boy, Teddy Roosevelt.

SPEAK SOFTLY, CARRY A BIG STICK, AND PLANT LOTS OF FUCKING TREES

Perhaps nobody epitomizes the graduating mindset better than the twenty-sixth president of the United States and personal idol of mine, Teddy Roosevelt.

For starters, Roosevelt was born with debilitating asthma. Rather than giving in to such a condition, which there would have been no shame in, he confronted it by embarking on an exceedingly active lifestyle.

Later on, Roosevelt endured the near-simultaneous deaths of his wife and mother, as they passed within eleven hours of each other when he was only twenty-six years of age. To symbolize the effect of this tragedy, Roosevelt wrote a large X in his diary on the day this happened, followed by the heartbreaking and solemn words "The light has gone out of my life."

Rather than continuing thoughts of despair and agony, Roosevelt dedicated his life to making a difference in the world. He graduated his mindset to achieve things few of us could even dream of. Just two years after the untimely passing of his wife and mother, Roosevelt became a member of the New York State Assembly and took on the specific challenge of battling corporate corruption.

After serving as assistant secretary of the Navy and governor of New York, Roosevelt won the election of 1901 to become president. He was reelected in the following election year and is still considered to have been one of the most successful presidents in American history.

Perhaps even more impressive than all his titles was Roosevelt's achievement as an environmentalist. He established the US Forest Service and five national parks, preserved 150 million acres of land, and is accredited with planting over three billion trees!

Take a moment to think about those accomplishments. Think deeply about how Roosevelt's life has impacted every one of us. If he hadn't taken that first step to graduate his mindset, moved on from the devastating losses he suffered, and dedicated himself to the country he loved and the planet he wanted to protect, we wouldn't have all those preserved sections of land to enjoy.

How many people have visited those national preserves that Roosevelt is responsible for?

How many people have been employed by the US Forest Service or one of the national parks he created?

How many people have breathed the fresh air that has been produced from the planting of over three billion trees?

Lastly, what would our country look like if this individual hadn't pushed himself to graduate, overcome, and accomplish so much?

Remember, the world needs your fucking ideas!

Chapter Four

ASK A LOT OF QUESTIONS

The art and science of asking questions is the source of all knowledge.
—PETER BERGER (AMERICAN-AUSTRIAN SOCIOLOGIST)

Ask plenty of questions because doing so is vital to your success as an entrepreneur. Accept the truth that other people know more about some things than you do. Nobody is born with an abundance of knowledge in everything, so rather than putting on a facade of expertise in all subjects, develop a thirst for knowledge and quench it with a constantly flowing stream of questioning.

UNDER A SEVEN-FOOT WING

Almost everything I needed to know about sales, I learned

many years ago from a talented salesman named Ron Holm. Ron was a Mormon and a rather imposing figure at seven feet tall with a white buzz cut, a somewhat standard set of black-framed glasses, and a striking baritone voice.

Kevin and I first met him when he was doing sales for a company that employed disabled individuals to assemble products. He approached us with the idea of having that company put together some of our smartphone cases.

Ron always started his talks with us by booming, "Gentlemen!" in a voice that sounded like it came from the love child of Morgan Freeman and the Allstate commercial guy. He followed up with a dramatic ten-second pause, and by the time he started speaking again, I was always shaking with anticipation, wondering what the fuck he was going to say next. It could have been anything. After that cliffhanger of a pause it seemed natural to then follow up with something like, "I'm going to have to crush your puny skulls with my massive, manly hands."

It turned out that what Ron had to say was usually quite friendly and disarming. It also didn't matter that he was as physically and audibly intimidating as a T. Rex; he would have been a sensational sales guy regardless, because he didn't rely on any bullshit intimidation tactics to close a sale. Rather, he used a refreshingly honest, inquisitive, and inherently decent approach to sales. Ron was a nice guy—almost a little too nice.

After working together for a while, he pulled us aside and said, "Gentlemen (dramatic ten-second pause), I wrote the foreword for a book that could teach you both a lot about sales. If you're interested, I'll give you a copy and teach you everything you need to know for free."

In one way, Ron was doing this out of the goodness of his giant heart, because he believed in our business, respected our mission, and wanted to see us succeed. But we also found out about a different reason much later.

ULTERIOR MOTIVES

Three or four months after Ron began mentoring us in the world of sales, he invited us to an event where he was speaking. We always thought of Ron as a righteous sort of guy, so we accepted his invitation. We figured it would be a sales conference or something very similar.

Fashionably late as usual, Kevin and I pulled up to the address Ron had given us. We stopped the car and looked around, but the only building in the immediate area was a church. "Odd place for a sales presentation," I said, and Kevin agreed, with a dismissive snicker.

Finally, we got out of the car and strolled up to the entrance where we thought we were going to meet Ron. The building was packed with people. Whatever event we were invited to must have been pretty important to have such a following in attendance.

We began walking down the aisle and the entire congregation turned their heads, staring at us as if it was our wedding day. I half expected to hear organ music as we worked our way to some seats. Then, we saw Ron at the front of the church, waving his bear-sized hands to get us to come join him in the front row with his wife and eleven children.

After a few minutes, the pastor showed up and performed an hour-long service. It seemed a lot longer, and I think Kevin and I both drifted off once or twice. Toward the end of the service, the pastor said, "And now, our brother Ron would like to say a few words and introduce some guests he told us about."

I thought, "Okay, maybe Ron is going to share some exciting news with the congregation about a new sales book he's writing or a course he's teaching at the community center." Still, I wasn't sure why he wanted us to be there, but it was his moment and we certainly didn't want to fuck it up for him, so we just applauded politely.

Ron gave a rather lengthy speech on the history of the

Church of Jesus Christ of Latter-day Saints. Just when I began to wonder when he was going to get to the fucking point, he transitioned into "Gentlemen (dramatic ten-second pause, as always), I've told everyone what a perfect fit you would be for our church. We'd all like to know if you would be so kind as to join our congregation?"

At that moment, Kevin and I looked at each other and slowly shook our heads side to side. Ron looked a little embarrassed, stared back out at the congregation, and tried to wrap up his speech.

I felt bad for Ron at that moment because he started scratching his head and looking as if he thought he had failed at recruiting us. It was a little sad, but there was no way Kevin and I were going to agree to convert to being Mormons on the spot.

It goes to show that even the best salespeople have limitations. Before Ron could go any further with his plea, and among a steady buzz of whispers from the crowd, Kevin and I bolted for the exit as fast as we could, jumped into the car, and tore out of there.

FEELING/FINDING QUESTIONS

Kevin and I escaped conversion into the LDS that night. Fortunately, we also kept all the great sales advice Ron had taught us, including the most valuable lesson, which was that you should never *try* to sell anything. Instead you should ask twenty to thirty feeling/finding questions. From there, the sale will almost close itself.

Feeling/finding questions are a way of getting information from your prospects to position your product or service as a solution to their most pressing problems. They allow you to develop an amicable relationship with your client while selling the product without seeming too pushy or salesy.

Let's say you're meeting with a buyer at a retail store to sell them your newly designed badminton racket. After you exchange introductions and pleasantries, you should follow up with some feeling/finding questions, as follows:

- So, tell me a little about your store.
- What's a normal product price for a badminton racket here?
- Is there a special style or color of badminton racket that sells really well?
- How many of those sales-leading rackets do you typically sell in a week?
- Are there any other products that sell particularly well?
- How often do you typically purchase your badminton rackets? Once a week? Once a month?

- What other companies do you buy rackets from, and why do you like working with them?

Learning this technique of question asking allowed us to sell the product not only to the big-box stores, but to other retailers as well. It basically allowed us to start the business and was the most important step in enabling us to sell our product.

Now take some time to think of ten to fifteen feeling/finding questions of your own and write them down on the lines below. As you're writing, think of the information you don't already have about your idea. Maybe it's questions around the industry, price points, or the global economic structure in that space; whatever it is, develop questions to ask experts who will provide those answers.

1. ....

2. ....

3. ....

4. ....

5. ....

6. ....

7. ....

8. ....

9. ....

10. ....

11. ....

12. ....

13. ....

14. ....

15. ....

Key Takeaway #5: At the end of the day, you need to be able to sell your idea. Otherwise it's just an idea, not a business. You have to figure out how somebody will be willing to pay money for your idea. Becoming a great question asker will enable you to get the information you need, from anyone, whenever you need it—and I definitely mean anyone.

When you're done asking your feeling/finding questions, use the information they give you to sell your own racket. The idea is to choose the answers that suit your product best and tailor your approach to those responses.

For example, if they tell you that blue badminton rackets for fifteen dollars apiece were the best sellers, you would tell the buyer, "Guess what? This is going to work amazingly well, because we have blue badminton rackets that sell for the same price, and people fucking love them! For now, we could send you a bunch of them every quarter and schedule some quick follow-up calls to see how they're selling. Sound good?"

In all seriousness, although Ron wasn't successful in converting us to his religion, he was tremendously successful in converting us into solid businesspeople with strong sales skills. You can learn a lot of the same lessons he taught us by reading *World Class Selling* by Roy Chitwood. Ron actually wrote the foreword for that book, and it's an excellent source for anyone looking for information related to sales. I highly recommend at least checking out the section about "Feeling/Finding Questions."

LEARN FROM THE BEST

Asking feeling/finding questions can be a great first step, but as the saying goes, "The more you know, the more you know," so ask questions of anybody who might know something you don't. Be humble in your approach. Find someone in any industry, or even a competitor, and say, "Hey, I don't know much about this, but I'd love to learn. You're clearly an expert here, so I have some questions, and I'd love it if you could help me out a little."

Honestly, almost every time I've used humility and honesty to ask another entrepreneur or business leader for help, it's worked. Think of some unique questions they've never been asked before, and they're likely to be impressed by your genuine curiosity and innovative thought process.

I first realized how well this could work when I met one of my idols, an absolute baller, Jay Strommen, who owns PD Instore, which is the company that makes all the presentation tables for Apple stores. This was the first big-time entrepreneur I had enough balls to approach—with a brief intro from a friend—and engage in a conversation. I had prepared for three to four days prior to meeting with him, and my goal was to pose questions that he had likely never heard before. When I finally met him, I seized the opportunity and asked questions about his business, personal life, and everything in between.

Interestingly enough, Jay was actually intrigued that someone was so captivated by what he was doing with his business and in his personal life. Overall, it was an awesomely impactful experience to talk to him. Since then, I've never been afraid to approach a major player in any industry with some questions that could help me to evolve.

Key Takeaway #6: Ask questions fearlessly! Finding people who can consistently help you to gain valuable knowledge is the key to continued growth as an entrepreneur and a person.

Chapter Five

BECOMING A POWERHOUSE THROUGH NETWORKING

—

You are the average of the five people you spend the most time with.

—JIM ROHN (AMERICAN ENTREPRENEUR, AUTHOR, AND MOTIVATIONAL SPEAKER)

So far, I've mentioned two impactful conversations I've had with two incredibly special people: Jay Strommen and Ken Rutkowski. Both of them are total ballers and have been mentors of mine for years now. My talk with Jay meant a lot to me personally and professionally because I greatly admire the way he lives and works. My talk with Ken occurred at a time in my life when all had seemed lost, as if my dreams were about to collapse.

He did more than just pat me on the back and tell me to keep fighting; he transformed my entire mindset. From that moment on, I began to see seemingly insurmountable challenges and fear of failure as opportunity and motivation.

Every time I spoke with Ken, it seemed like I learned something. I felt the same way each time I spoke with another positive and influential person in my life, Nanxi Liu, a serial entrepreneur. When I realized how valuable my time with them was, I decided to make a conscious effort to spend as much time with them as possible.

I wasn't exactly great friends with either of them at first, but I knew they represented a lot of the lifestyle I wanted to manifest. I admired the way they talked with people, the way they ran their businesses, the way they did almost everything. So, anytime I had an extra few hundred dollars or was able to find a cheap plane ticket, I flew to California to hang out with one or both of them. It was my way of networking.

I would usually crash on a friend's couch or figure out some temporary living arrangement. Honestly, I barely even had enough money to buy food at that point. (Yes, this is post-Trish time.) The bottom line is, I didn't worry about logistics very much. I simply knew that I needed to soak up more of how they lived their lives, so I did whatever I could to enable more of their overall awesomeness to sink into my own life.

Ken is a human high-voltage generator. He calls himself a super networker, but he's so much more than that. Presently, he runs an entrepreneurial group I belong to, called METal International. At this point, he's made enough money to last the rest of his life, so his sole purpose is to help others achieve the life they desire. To do this, he connects people from all over the world who can benefit from each other's skillsets and ambitions.

Ken also has a radio show where he talks to some of the biggest names in business. His mannerisms and style of communication are so incredible that he gets billionaires from all industries to appear on his show and open up about their businesses and personal lives. Everybody loves to interact with Ken. He makes friends instantly with his contagious enthusiasm and playful humor.

Dogsledding with my entrepreneurship group in the Arctic, Svalbard (The dogs were actually extremely lazy and we ended up walking halfway up the mountain.)

Nanxi has out-of-this-world intelligence going for her. She started a biomedical company in college that kept vaccines cold without using ice or dry ice. Her company was tremendously successful; in fact, it exploded—financially, not chemically.

From there, she went on to start a company called Enplug that offers software for digital displays to cycle information for businesses. They provide real-time social media interaction between brands and users. Nanxi has also started a hedge fund for cryptocurrency. Don't ask me to explain that one, because I get a headache just thinking about it. I told you she was smart.

Beyond her superior intelligence, however, I noticed how Nanxi ran her businesses, particularly the way she empowered her team of engineers. She didn't get bogged down in the minutiae of daily operations when she didn't need to.

Nanxi put a lot of work into the hiring process, which ensured she had incredibly talented people working for her, and then she let them shine. It helped me to realize that I didn't have to get on the ground floor every day to show people how to do every fucking aspect of their jobs. In fact, they probably knew how to do them better than I did anyway. Nanxi taught me all about empowerment, which was an extremely valuable lesson.

As a result of my efforts to connect more deeply with Ken and Nanxi, I've benefited from a lot of valuable insight from incredible people over the years. Although we weren't super close friends at first, I consider them to be two of my very best friends today.

THE CONSCIOUS CIRCLE

As I began to see the positive impact that spending more time with Ken and Nanxi was having on my business and personal life, I took the concept a little further. I began to wonder, "What if I surrounded myself with more people like that?"

Suddenly, that idea started to take shape into a form of networking I call the "conscious circle." What I mean by that is to look around at the people you're spending the most time with. They could be family, friends, or coworkers, or maybe they're the people who make your skinny vanilla latte every morning at the neighborhood coffee shop. Ask yourself if those people are helping you to become the person you aspire to be.

Through that thought process, I realized that I needed more of what Ken and Nanxi were doing for me, and less of some of the other relationships I was a part of. That's when the words of highly influential entrepreneur Jim Rohn started to resonate. Those words, which lead off this chapter—"You are the average of the five people you spend the most time with"—meant that I should make a conscious effort to ensure that the primary people I spent time with were the ones who could help me grow to become the kind of entrepreneur, leader, and person I wanted to be.

The first thing I noticed when I began that exercise was that, in my opinion, five people wasn't enough to form a complete conscious circle, so I extended Jim Rohn's concept to include seven people.

Developing your conscious circle is about taking control of your own destiny. It's about knowing who you want to become in life and making consistently good choices to allow that to happen. You don't have to abandon anybody, but you might have to spend less time with old friends and acquaintances to accomplish bigger and better things in your life and for the world around you. The point is, you don't have to be a dick about it.

THE CIRCLE EVOLVES

Approximately one year before I started writing this book, I noticed one thing in particular that was missing from my conscious circle. Faith had always been a big part of my life. Through journaling, I realized that I wasn't as connected to it as I wanted to be.

Journaling is a great way to check yourself. By recording the various happenings in your life—both significant and somewhat routine—you give yourself checkpoints to reference. Those checkpoints can tell you if you're on track for certain goals and objectives. By looking through my journal, I realized that my conscious circle was missing a spiritual presence.

I found that spiritual presence in an amazing psychologist and life coach named Kathleen. A friend of a friend introduced us a few years ago, and since then she has added immense value to my spirituality and mindset. I still talk to her three to four times per month, and she does an excellent job of keeping me on track with becoming the person I want to be and become.

One of the things she most helped me with was gratitude. Listening to her perspective on the connectedness of humanity and the gifts this world gives us made me so much more grateful for every damned thing I see and feel. With that sentiment working its way through my mindset, I started a new ritual, which is to announce something I'm grateful for before every meal.

Christians are very familiar with this custom and refer to it as "saying grace." But I feel like sometimes the value of it gets lost in ritualistic prayer, which can become a repetition of words that have been recited a million times and provide little actual meaning. Rather than regurgitate a formal prayer that was written thousands of years ago, I like to say some words off the top of my head about something I'm truly grateful for, and I encourage others I'm sharing the meal with to do the same. It's cool with me if they choose not to, but I always like to extend an invitation just in case.

Putting God back into my life was a conscious decision I made about a year prior to writing this book, and it's had a profoundly positive impact on me ever since. Finding

God again through journaling and graduating my mindset has brought me much closer to the person I want to become.

Spirituality can be an important component of your life as well, whether or not you believe in God. If spirituality is important to you, or if you feel it's missing in your life, make sure there is someone in your conscious circle to help you with it.

Key Takeaway #7: Your conscious circle is—hands down—the seven most important decisions you will continuously make in your life. An individual in that close circle truly has the ability to help you achieve the extent of your dreams. On the flip side, they can also keep you stuck in a comfortable life forever and never allow you to achieve anything beyond your current state of complacency. Keep in mind, your conscious circle will evolve, so it's a good idea to revisit your list at least once per year.

For some people like myself, spirituality is a necessary component. Others may feel compelled to get closer to social or political causes, environmentalism, or volunteerism. There's a whole world of choices out there to identify with. Finding people to positively impact you with any of them could bring you much closer to the person you want to become.

CHECK YOURSELF

Take some time to develop your own conscious circle. Start by writing on the lines below the names of the seven people you currently interact with most on a daily basis.

OLD CONSCIOUS CIRCLE

1. ....

2. ....

3. ....

4. ....

5. ....

6. ....

7. ....

Now, think about the people who are already in your life or the people you want in your life who could help you to get closer to the person you want to become. Take a few minutes to seriously think about this. If necessary, take a break for a week or two and come back to it. Once you have those names in your head, take some additional time to ask yourself some critically important follow-up questions:

Are these seven people the accumulation of who I want to become?

Are these seven people going to push me to accomplish my dreams?

Are these seven people going to support me through thick and thin?

Can I call any one of them at any time and be confident that they'll answer my call?

Am I supporting these people the way I want to be supported?

Humans lean toward complacency and comfort, so the answer is likely no. If that's the case, you need to make some adjustments to that circle for a kick start to personal and professional growth. Again, it doesn't mean you have to be a dick about it and completely forget your oldest and dearest friends.

If this exercise causes you to discover that certain people in your life are predominantly negative influences, you'll need to remove that sort of toxicity somehow. That could be really fucking hard, but necessary, because toxic relationships can make it nearly impossible to achieve everything you want in life. You may not need to disassociate yourself entirely, but you'll need to minimize your exposure to them, at the very least.

There may be other relationships that aren't necessarily toxic but aren't as beneficial as those in your conscious circle. You may be forced to spend less time with those people as well, because it may be the only way to free up enough of your schedule to spend the appropriate amount of time with your most positive influencers.

Now, curate your new conscious circle.

Who are the seven people who are going to push, challenge, and support you to accomplish your dreams and goals? Don't stop until you come up with seven people. (No offense to Jim Rohn, but five people is just a blip on the social radar for most of us.)

Now, write down your new list of positive influencers. Next to their names, write down specifically what you most admire and appreciate about them. Then list what you want to learn and attract from them as well.

NEW CONSCIOUS CIRCLE

1. ....

2. ....

3. ....

4. ....

5. ....

6. ....

7. ....

Remember, it's your life and it's up to you to live it the way you want.

Chapter Six

SOMETIMES YOU HAVE TO BE AN ASSHOLE

Sometimes you have to be selfish to be selfless.
—EDWARD ALBERT (AMERICAN ACTOR)

There's a popular expression that describes the native citizens of Minnesota and Wisconsin. It's called *Minnesota Nice*. For the most part, it does a good job of describing us. We are pretty nice people in general. Unless, of course, you include the globally unprecedented amount of passive aggressiveness that exists in the region, which can definitely make things not so nice. Another expression I've often heard is *nice guys finish last*. I don't buy into that one completely. You can be a nice guy and accomplish plenty of personal goals and objectives. In a lot of ways, being *nice* can be a valuable personal attribute.

The cold hard truth, however, is that sometimes you have to be an asshole.

SELFISH VERSUS SELFLESS

Minnesota Nice means that, regardless of your innermost feelings toward someone, you should always be kind, help others, and do the right thing. Growing up, I was taught that even if I intensely disliked someone, disagreed with their morals, or just straight-up thought they were a bad person, I should never show it in public.

To become an entrepreneur, I learned that I had to transition from *Minnesota Nice* to being an asshole when necessary. To do this effectively, I wrestled mightily with the differences between being selfish and being selfless. According to Merriam-Webster, the following are precise definitions of both terms:

Selfish *(adjective, \\'self-ish\\)* Concerned excessively or exclusively with oneself: seeking or concentrating on one's own advantage, pleasure, or well-being without regard for others.

Selfless *(adjective, \\'sel-fləs\\)* Having no concern for oneself: unselfish.

The key differentiating factor between these terms is perspective. An act that could be viewed as selfish by some people in certain situations could also be seen as selfless by other people. For example, consider the following story about a complex and mostly toxic relationship I had with an ex-girlfriend.

AM I A HUMANITARIAN OR AN ASSHOLE?

Shortly after my girlfriend and I had arrived home from a trip to Italy, I had another travel destination already in the works. The opportunity had arisen for me to go to Europe to work on some tree-planting partnerships with various socially responsible and globally respected businesses. I viewed it as a path for me to execute at a high level on something I was passionate about. By going there, I would be a big part of a key initiative to fund and plant hundreds of thousands of trees all over the world. That was my big-picture focus, and it seemed to me like a pretty selfless endeavor. However, that's not how she saw it.

I was going to surprise her with the tickets to Europe, where she would join me in this amazing opportunity. Right or wrong, she saw it as more selfish than anything else. Perhaps she was looking at the situation through a very small lens. She said, "How could you expect me to just drop everything and go to Europe with you, so you can work? Did it even occur to you that I might have something going on at the same time and you should check with me before booking anything?"

I thought about that and realized that she had a good point. From her perspective, it was a selfish request on my part. From the larger perspective, however, I viewed it as a selfless journey to undertake. I thought of it as sacrificing my own personal comfort for the sake of the greater good. Rather than staying at home with my girlfriend and participating in all the activities we love, we would be going overseas to help the planet.

By planting trees all over Europe, we would be providing a healthier environment for generations to come. Traveling and reforesting the planet was never something I was focused on for personal gain. Rather, I wanted to make our planet a better place for my future children and build a company that would support them. It was a perfect example of how two people could see the same situation from completely different perspectives.

That relationship ended badly, and I was crushed at the time. Now, however, I see where its dissolution was a blessing, because we didn't see eye to eye on a lot of similar issues. Our perspectives were vastly differently in many ways.

I ended up going on that trip and doing some incredible

work that contributed greatly to the health of our planet. One hundred years from today, entire communities will benefit from those trees I planted. Also, many hardworking individuals will have earned a good income from the jobs I helped to create while I was there.

Ultimately, I made the decision that I needed to be a little selfish in my personal life to act more holistically selfless. Long ago, I decided my mission was to plant more trees than one of my personal idols, Teddy Roosevelt. That goal isn't a selfish one; it's a part of a calling I feel like I've been given by a higher power. I understand that goal will require me to be *selfish* many more times in my life to create something truly amazing for future generations. That trip to Europe would contribute greatly to making that dream a reality.

My ex-girlfriend just couldn't see the bigger picture, and that's okay because it's something a lot of people struggle with. Not that either one of us was necessarily right or wrong, but the situation was probably indicative of how different we really were as people.

Key Takeaway #8: Many visionaries and entrepreneurs sacrifice their dreams for a significant other who doesn't see the bigger picture. Ensure your special someone supports your idea to change the world. Chances are this individual is part of your conscious circle because they're obviously a huge part of your life. Therefore, their support is undeniably necessary. If you know you're on the right track, or on the way to achieving your true calling, don't let anyone get in the way of that vision—ever.

Now I've got another story that involves a much larger group of people who also failed to see the bigger picture in a critical situation. In this case, I had no choice but to make a brutally unpopular decision to fire an extremely well-liked individual in my company—further proof that sometimes you have to be an asshole.

SEE THE BIGGER PICTURE

A few years ago, we hired this super nice family man named Josh to be our operations leader. He was a great fit for our corporate culture because he shared a lot of our corporate values.

Personally, I had a lot of respect for Josh as a human being. Unfortunately, he could not get the fucking job done. Josh had a lot of experience at managing big teams in enterprise-level corporations, but he had no experience managing small teams of ten to twenty people, which involves a totally different dynamic.

Josh's Achilles' heel was likely that he was too damned nice. Everybody loved him, but nobody would bust their ass for him. I remember one time walking by and seeing one of his team members sitting on a chair, sanding a component with her feet up on the countertop, in a relax and laidback position. A little dumbfounded, I decided to stay and watch how long it took for her to sand that piece. She didn't notice me watching, but it took her over ten minutes to do something that should have taken about seven seconds. To be fair, she was texting for about five minutes in between the start and finish of the sanding process, so interpret the total time wasted accordingly.

That particular incident wasn't the only time I witnessed an extreme level of operational inefficiency under Josh's supervision. Before long, I realized that Josh was too nice to get people to perform the way we needed them to. We had given him plenty of opportunities to turn things around and had put him on official performance plans, but he still wasn't able to get the job done, so I had to make a tough decision. I had to be an asshole. Realistically, I had no other choice. The only options were the following:

1. **Be a nice guy:** Continue the current state of operational inefficiency and let the company sink due to poor performance. I viewed this as the selfish decision to make because it makes my job easy. All I have to do is let the company roll on to its collision course with self-destruction. Everybody remains my friend and no one gets singled out as incompetent.

2. **Be an asshole:** By firing Josh, which would be a horribly unpopular decision, we'd be able to save the company. This way, the other twenty or so employees would keep their jobs and we'd continue our mission to have a positive global impact on the environment. I saw this as the selfless choice, but it's strange how alone I was in that perspective.

Eventually, I wisely chose door number two and decided to let Josh go. It was an incredibly hard decision because he was an awesome dude, but it was clearly the right thing to do for everybody's well-being, including Josh. It wouldn't have been doing him any favors to keep him in a job he sucked at. By letting him move on to a job with an opportunity to succeed, we were helping him.

Plus, it wasn't like we made the decision on the spur of the moment. We'd spoken with Josh on other occasions, but he still wasn't able to turn things around. What we didn't foresee, however, was that the rest of the company would react so poorly.

IF HE GOES, I GO, AND I GO, AND I GO…

We fired Josh on a Sunday, which seemed like the best day to do it, because at least it didn't ruin the guy's weekend and he didn't have to show up Monday morning to suffer the indignity of cleaning out his desk in front of everybody.

Despite our best efforts to keep Josh's termination on the down low until we could inform everyone, word still got out before our Monday morning meeting. During the meeting, Ross, one of Josh's subordinates, got up and said, "You know what? I don't think you guys know what the fuck you're doing. I completely disagree with letting Josh go and I quit!"

The worst part about that little temper tantrum was that it could have been articulated much more effectively. If Ross had asked to talk to me in my office—one-on-one—rather than trying to show me up in front of the entire company, we probably could have worked something out that would have been much more beneficial to everyone. As a matter of fact, I had planned on having Ross take over Josh's management position!

Instead, what happened was this: one by one, all of Josh's team members stood up, told me what an asshole I was, how I didn't know how to run the company, and quit. In total, fourteen people walked out the door that day and never came back. There was even one dude named Emmit who not only didn't work for Josh, but didn't even know who the fuck Josh was! He just wanted to be one of the cool kids.

The biggest kick in the ass about Emmit leaving that day was that I had taken a chance on hiring him in the first place. Previously, he'd worked at a Jimmy John's franchise and moonlighted as a valet attendant for a local restaurant. I went to dinner at the restaurant one night, handed him my keys on the way out, and saw him haul ass to get my car. I was so impressed by how fast he went to get my car that I figured he must have had a damned good work ethic, so I offered him a job!

Emmit took the job immediately and then walked out the door with everybody else just a couple of months later.

I actually tried to stop everybody in the middle of their insanity to make sure they were fully aware of what they were doing. Knowing that most of them were living paycheck to paycheck, I knew they couldn't afford to just quit without having another job lined up. I said, "Guys, guys, guys! Do you understand that by quitting, you're not getting any more money? This means you get no unemployment. You get that, right?"

Truthfully, I'm sure that the kid who didn't know Josh had no idea what he was getting into, but that was on him because I tried to warn him. Another thing I doubt any of them understood was that if I hadn't let Josh go, I would have needed to let them all go in a few weeks, because the company was suffering greatly from their collective suboptimal output.

As all of this turmoil was taking place, I suddenly realized that another guy—Mitch Brandes—was starting his first day on the job. After fourteen people walked out, there were only a few of us left, including Mitch. I turned to Mitch and said, "Well, how about that for your first few hours of work? Looks like we're going to need you to step up pretty quickly into a management roll, so I'm looking forward to working with you!"

Turned out that hiring Mitch in the first place was one of the best things I ever did. He's still our production manager today and has been nothing short of amazing since he's been with us.

After the not-so-subtle demonstration, I did my best to rally the remaining troops, whatever was left of them. I said, "So, we're obviously in a really shitty situation here. It's not going to be easy, but we need to come together. I promise I'll never forget it if you agree to hang in with me here. We're all going to work really fucking hard for the next few weeks until we find good people to replace the ones who just left."

IT'S ALL ABOUT THE *WHY*

The people that walked out that day obviously didn't see the bigger picture. Conversely, the people who stuck around were there for more than just a job. They still wanted to build quality products, create jobs in the US, and bring nature back into people's lives. Some of them—like Mitch—are still with me today, and I'm incredibly thankful for their tireless efforts ever since.

Once again, I'm compelled to think that what kept those people around was that they believed in the *why* of my business just as strongly as I did. If my only intentions behind Josh's dismissal were in fattening my own wallet, I would have truly been an asshole in that situation. But that clearly wasn't the case. I still wanted to build quality American products, create more jobs, and bring nature back into people's lives. However, the only way I was going to execute that mission was to cut the cord with someone who, despite the best of intentions, was pulling the team in the opposite direction.

Watching those fourteen individuals call me an asshole and walk out the door may have even strengthened my resolve. It also made me realize how deeply I could trust the loyalty of my remaining team members. For that reason, I believe that trust and loyalty are two of the biggest attributes you should look for when hiring your own team.

The next chapter includes a story that is hilarious, yet terrifying at the same time. The takeaway, however, is that it completely supports the value of trust and loyalty in business and in life. After all, there's nothing quite like spending time in a Malagasy prison with someone to validate the trust in your relationship with them.

The Beginning of BUY ONE. PLANT ONE.® (Yes, this is my dog, Angel. No, she is not good at planting trees.)

Chapter Seven

GOOD FRIENDS GET YOU OUT OF JAIL; BEST FRIENDS ARE IN THE CELL WITH YOU

Teamwork begins by building trust. And the only way to do that is to overcome our need for invulnerability.

—PATRICK LENCIONI (AMERICAN AUTHOR
AND BUSINESS MANAGEMENT EXPERT)

Loyalty and trust will always be two of the most important factors I look for in business and in life. Nine times out of ten, I will choose to hire or do business with someone I trust completely over someone I trust mostly. We all make the occasional hiring blunder, but I should probably raise the bar of that statement to ten times out of ten.

The importance of trust and loyalty was strengthened when I experienced those fourteen people walking out on my company. It was solidified by another far more extreme incident.

ROGER THAT

One of the most extraordinary trips I've ever taken was a tree-planting mission in the rural, distressed parts of Madagascar.

When we arrived in the island nation, we had a lot of work to do, but we were happy to do it. The landscape in Madagascar can vary tremendously depending on the region, so we had to use different modes of transportation to get the job done. Sometimes we used helicopters to fly into extremely remote villages. Other times we took canoes to paddle across rivers and streams to the designated planting zone.

The "canoes" we used were of the makeshift variety. Most of the time, they were nothing more than hollowed-out logs with gaping holes in them. We constantly had to bail water out of those things to keep them afloat as we paddled. The good thing is that when the waters you're paddling in are infested with poisonous snakes, you tend to both paddle and bail out water very quickly.

International Tree Planting Program (Pre-Malagasy Prison Time)

Transit to Local Planting Locations, Madagascar (Made of shitty logs that leak several gallons per minute)

When we got to the specific area for planting, we quickly got down to business, working on partnerships, education of the tribes, and overall implementation of the tree nurseries and programs. We typically tried to get the hell out of there before any of the criminal element from the neighboring ghettos could threaten us or the mission. Sometimes that was a lot easier said than done.

The terrain in one particular region included a lot of bumpy dirt roads and rocky terrain, so we rode four-wheelers to get in and out of the planting areas.

A chairman for one of the nonprofits and my new best friend on the trip, Roger, and I were riding our four-wheelers back one night when fate took a funny yet scary and dangerous twist. Before I go any further with this story, understand that Roger was about fifty years old with a total dad bod. He was a great guy, but not someone you would team up with for a street fight in a third-world country, unless he had a machine gun, which unfortunately he did not.

It was hot as hell on this fateful evening. The dust was kicking up everywhere and sticking to us like flies caught in a spiderweb. We were cruising along side by side at about thirty miles per hour on a dirt road, desperately wanting nothing more than to get back to our rooms to unwind. We were super tired from a long day of hard work, when all of a sudden—*smash!*

Roger's four-wheeler got completely T-boned by some woman driving a car from out of nowhere. The four-wheeler went flying in one direction and Roger went hurtling through the thick sun-drenched air in another. My first reaction was "Holy fucking shit, Roger's dead!"

We were in the middle of East Bumfuck, Madagascar, about two to three miles from the closest village. I stopped my four-wheeler to check on Roger, half expecting to see his arms and legs bent and twisted in all different and unnatural directions. To make matters worse, the woman who hit him was at this point out of her car, screaming something at me in Malagasy and charging at me aggressively.

As if things weren't bad enough, all the yelling and

screaming this crazy woman was doing somehow caught the attention of a bunch of other Malagasy natives who just happened to be walking down the middle of the road to nowhere. Before I realized what was going on, the crowd had turned into an angry mob and had formed a circle around us, making sure we couldn't escape.

The good news was that Roger wasn't dead. He was, however, severely banged up, with scratches and bruises all over him. Before long, another guy showed up in an old beat-up Nissan Maxima with a couple of rims missing and a broken taillight. He was dressed in sweatpants and a maroon beret. Turns out this guy was some sort of police officer.

As I was checking on Roger, I looked over my shoulder and saw this woman blatantly run up to the officer and hand him cash. Almost immediately after that, two other fully uniformed officers arrived. They had the same maroon berets on, but these guys had batons and looked like they had walked straight off the set of the movie *Blood Diamond*. I thought to myself, "This is not fucking good. We could be in a hell of a lot of trouble here."

One of the officers actually spoke some broken English, but what he had to say wasn't good. I tried telling him that the psychopath who hit us clearly gave the other guy some payoff money. He looked at me as if to say, "D'uh, that's what we do around here, dumbass American!" Instead, he grabbed me by the arm and rather persuasively insisted, "You're both coming with me."

I tried to negotiate with him, but he wasn't having any of it. I told him to look at the tire tracks and he could easily see that this woman had almost killed my friend. All that accomplished was a shouting match, and the guys with the batons usually win that sort of thing.

The officers propped both of us up against the four-wheelers, patted us down, and searched us. After that, they threw us into the back seat of one of their rent-a-cop–looking police cars and drove about twenty minutes until we got to a cluster of ransacked buildings.

During that ride, I was trying to figure out how somebody would find us, and I couldn't come up with anything plausible. I started to think we were going to end up as two people who went on a trip overseas and never came back.

Finally, the rent-a-cop police car stopped, and the officers walked us past a gate into an open courtyard. There were a few old motorcycles and junk cars scattered around and a bunch of other guys—some with similar maroon berets—just hanging out. One of them was drinking a beer and others were smoking cigarettes. It looked a lot like a scene from the movie *Mad Max*. Just picture a Mexican courtyard in the middle of the desert with a broken-down, old building in it that's occupied by all sorts of questionable characters with the look of bad intentions all over their faces.

Our escorts kept walking us toward a dilapidated two-story structure with busted windows. Inside, they stopped at a desk in the middle of the room that was stacked at least a foot high with paper. There was one guy sitting there stoically, stamping one paper after another. He spoke with the guards and pointed to an empty room off to the side.

They walked us to a fifteen-by-fifteen room that reeked of unknown origins—urine, maybe, or some other bodily fluid. It smelled like a whiff of death. The walls were an unsightly mixture of broken stucco and dirt. Another guy was in there at a desk, also stoically stamping papers. There was no electricity, no lights.

The operation appeared pretty half-assed to me. The doors were wide open and nobody seemed to be paying much attention to Roger and me. For a moment, I thought I could have easily run out the back door and be long gone before anyone noticed, but what would happen to Roger, I wondered. I decided there was no way I was leaving Roger behind. Not only wouldn't I leave anyone to such an unknown and potentially horrible fate, but I definitely wasn't going to do that to such a genuinely good dude.

I'm the type of person who constantly assesses every situation. I was thinking that I was a solid wrestler and decently trained in jujitsu, so I started playing out the possibilities of various situations in my mind, like what would happen if I grabbed their batons or used other objects in the room to try to fight my way through these people. Every way it played out, however, resulted in a bad outcome. After all, we were severely outnumbered and I had a wounded soldier with a dad bod to account for, so we were officially up shit creek in Madagascar without a paddle.

After I came to the conclusion that there would be no man left behind that day, I started to think about other possibilities. The guy who was stamping papers in this room looked like he murdered people for a living, so I was fearful of that. He had this look on his face that he didn't care about anything, especially not these two pasty-faced, overprivileged, tree-planting Americans.

Eventually, a couple of other officers came over and tried to communicate with us. We began to tell our story, but nothing worked. They just stared blankly, as if they had already decided what was going to happen to us.

Meanwhile, unbeknownst to anyone else, I had a GoPro in my hands, which had been folded in my lap the whole time. When I realized we weren't getting anywhere by talking to these guys, I decided to click it on, figuring if we were going to die, we were at least going to get it recorded. I didn't realize, however, that the sound was up and when I clicked the power button, it made a loud beeping sound.

When that happened, one of the officers grabbed me by the shirt and yelled something unrecognizable at me in Malagasy. The GoPro fell onto the seat and everybody got heated about it. Roger was yelling at them, they were yelling at us, and all I could think was that they were going to cut our fucking hands off or make us eat the GoPro like a group of Russian mob bosses from the sixties.

Finally, the guy who had grabbed me threw me back onto my chair. Another guy grabbed the GoPro, placed it on his desk, and alternated glances between us and the GoPro, as if to say, "What the fuck do you think you're doing with this thing?"

This place was in the middle of nowhere. They could have simply killed us and nobody would ever know. I was trying to come to terms with our fate, looking out this broken window, when, like some sort of modern miracle, I saw one of our tree-planting buddies walking by right outside. "Are you fucking kidding me?" I said to myself. I waved at him and called under my breath, "Psst. Josy! Roger and I are about to get our fucking hands cut off in here. Please come help us!"

Somehow, I got Josy's attention. Moments later, he walked through the doorway as if he owned the place, passing by all the guards like a king as they nodded to him. As it turned out, Josy was highly influential in that village; everybody knew him.

He started shooting the shit with these dudes like they were old college roommates. It was like a switch was flipped. Their facial expressions went from menacing murderers to kindly comrades. They clicked on the GoPro and began recording the amicable conversation that ensued. They even included Roger and me in their friendly exchange.

After we all became best buddies, the Malagasy officers took us back to the scene of the accident and we reconstructed the incident for them. The mood became so lightened that they even laughed when I described to them how Roger flew like Superman about thirty feet in the air. In a bizarre turn of events, they tracked down the lady who had caused the accident and arrested her.

When it was all over, Josy said, "Yeah guys, that was close to ending very, very badly for you. You are stupidly lucky that I happened to walk by when I did."

LOYALTY AND TRUST ABOVE ALL ELSE

That situation could have ended much differently had either of us decided to make a run for it. Either or both of us could have been killed or beaten or left to languish in a Malagasy jail.

Two things prevented those scenarios from taking place: loyalty and trust. Fortunately, Roger and I had established a bond while working together. Since then, I've learned that it's far better for me to hire someone I trust 100 percent, even if they have only half the skillset of another candidate.

YOU'RE HIRED! NOW HELP ME SAVE THE COMPANY

My theory of seeking trust in the people I hire was proven right by two of my team members—John Guenveur and Gerard Garramone—who exemplify this notion perhaps better than anyone else.

Several years ago, the fate of WOODCHUCK was in jeopardy. The company was not in a good financial position and we needed to borrow more money from the bank if we were going to make it. The business was suffering from a lack of annual consistency. We enjoyed heavy fourth quarters, but our business slowed drastically for the rest of the year. By the time Q3 rolled around that fateful year, we had run into some particularly bad cash-flow problems.

We had a couple of large orders on the horizon that were going to save us, but we needed cash to make it to that point. I asked John and Gerard to make a ninety-minute trip with me to visit the bank and ask for an additional $200,000 to get the company through Q3.

John had been with the company for a while, but Gerard was in maybe his second or third week with us. Either one of them could have easily bailed at that point, especially Gerard. I would have completely understood if either one of them said something like, "You know, this just doesn't sound like a good situation. I'm out."

That's not what either one of them did, however. They both sucked it up like the kick-ass, go-to team players they have always been and went into battle with me. We presented the bank with our best pitch, which was all about our *why* once again.

John and Gerard helped me to explain what we had already done. We had planted about a half million trees across the world and were damned proud of it. That wasn't all we talked about. We went on to explain how deeply we believed in our ability to build quality American products and how we relished the thought of employing honest, like-minded, hardworking Americans to do it.

John and Gerard rocked that presentation so hard that

the bank granted our request. They gave us the money we needed to fill those upcoming orders, and we celebrated with food and beer at a restaurant across the street. Shortly after we sat down there to pat each other on the back for a job well done, we received a phone call to fill one of the largest orders we had ever received. WOODCHUCK was about to take off, and it was all due to the trust and loyalty of the people around me—proof positive that in addition to those two key elements, teamwork will take your business to new heights.

Key Takeaway #9: Find trustworthy and loyal people to be on your team. This should be a rule with no exceptions.

Chapter Eight

THE COLLECTIVE IS BETTER THAN THE INDIVIDUAL

Great things in business are never done by one person; they're done by a team of people.
—STEVE JOBS (CEO AND COFOUNDER OF APPLE)

I've personally witnessed the catastrophic failures that can occur due to being surrounded by bad people. On the other end of the spectrum, I've also seen what's possible when good people stick together through loyalty and trust. It's beautiful and inspirational, and I'm happy to share a couple of stories about that experience in this chapter. The first one starts with my quirky, creative, and awesome team at WOODCHUCK.

Let's start with some of the people you're already familiar with.

NOT-SO-ORDINARY PEOPLE

John is the VP of sales, who has been with the company for about four years now. Occasionally, he shows up for work in a button-down shirt, but usually you'll see him wearing flip-flops and gym shorts. Does it matter? Fuck no, because he's a sales ninja in the B2B world. I'm not sure how he does it, but he usually works until around three in the morning and comes back to the office around seven. It's probably not a working formula for everybody, but for John it absolutely is.

Gerard is now our president. He's around forty-two years old but looks like he's in his late twenties. He has a unique way of consistently getting the best out of people. He gets great results and has an amazing knack for helping team members grow within their roles at the company and as people.

From just looking at Gerard, you might think he's in a kick-ass rock band. Instead, he runs a wood products manufacturing company in the humble little state of Minnesota—not quite the same scale from a perspective of fame and fortune, but he is awesome at what he does for us.

Mitch, who saw fourteen people quit on his first day, now runs our operations department. It's kind of strange that he started at a time that was so symbolic of people who clearly didn't see the bigger picture of our business. Mitch got it from day one. He can usually be seen buzzing around the office with earbuds or talking on the phone about a shipping situation. His talent for making things happen from a production standpoint is truly amazing.

I consider myself incredibly fortunate to have such amazing people around me all the time, supporting WOODCHUCK's mission and helping me to change the world. It's hard to image where I'd be without them, particularly my right-hand man, Alex Jones.

Alex prefers to operate behind the scenes, but he just may be the most important person in the company. He is an incredible asset and perfectly exemplifies the caring, loyal, dedicated individual I look for in all the people I onboard. From ensuring tax documentation and paperwork is submitted on time to fending off unwanted visitors and ensuring I stick to my schedule, Alex is the man that helps me be the best I can be.

These people and just about everyone else on my team have two big common character traits. First, they're all a little quirky in their own special way. I don't fit the typical businessperson mold. I like to think creatively and do some crazy things, so that's what I look for when assembling my team.

LET YOUR FREAK FLAG FLY!

One of our company mottos is to "let your freak flag fly." That's our way of supporting a corporate culture that encourages outside-the-box innovation and creative thinking. We're not just assembling widgets all day and filling out budget reports. My team is always thinking about how to do things better, and I love that about them.

It doesn't hurt that the second thing my team has in common is that they're also awesome at their jobs. You wouldn't necessarily look at me or my team and immediately think, "Yeah, that's a multimillion-dollar business right there." But we are. Collectively, our ragtag group of variously fucked-up individuals works incredibly well together, despite our unorthodox style.

In addition to letting our freak flags fly, we also proudly display our one-hundred-year manifesto at the front doorway of our headquarters. This lets people see who we are and why we do what we do. It expresses our collective mission for the next one hundred years. Manufacturing wood products is not found anywhere in that manifesto. Rather, it focuses on our unified, intense passion for putting nature back into people's lives.

The manifesto is direct and contains a few curse words, so it's not for everybody. But that's okay, because it tells people right away how we operate. Prospective employees get an immediate feel for our corporate culture. From there, they can make their own decision on whether or not they're a good fit. It's fine if you're offended or don't agree with anything in that manifesto, but in that case this might not be the right place for you to work.

100 YEAR MANIFESTO

How did you change the world today?

We're here to leave the WORLD a better place.

*We're here to INSPIRE others to experience
THE WONDER OF NATURE.*

EVERY DAY you'll have an impact.

BEAST MODE

We're here to MAKE SHIT HAPPEN. We're DREAMERS, doers, and

*STRATEGIC thinkers. We are the people
changing the world EVERY day.*

*We're constantly driven to learn and improve,
and are always elevating our*

*mindset, even when we're number one. We
have a focused insanity on our*

goals. We are Beast Mode.

PREMIUM

*Premium is not an end result; it is our
truth. It starts with an idea and*

*continues beyond delivery. It's in every
experience we create. It's the reason*

we push so hard, sacrifice so much, and constantly strive

to be 10 steps ahead of the best.

NO FUCKING BOUNDARIES

*You can change the world if you challenge
the status quo. You can't change*

*the WORLD if you are a bobblehead. Yell a little, show your passion,
and communicate however you need to make the world a better plae.*

Embrace the best version of yourself; be AUTHENTIC.

If we wanted to be normal, we wouldn't be here.

We are Beast Mode.

We are Premium.

We have No Fucking Boundaries.

We are WOODCHUCK.

The Woodchuck Manifesto

I suggest you do the same thing with your business. Don't hide who you are or what you stand for just because it may be a little unorthodox or some people may not agree with it. Remember, you can't please all of the people all of the time, so why fucking bother?

If you need a little help writing a manifesto that fits your business, I recommend reading the book *Traction*, by Gino Wickman. There's some great information in there to get you started.

Key Takeaway #10: Embrace whatever makes you or your business unique. For example, if you believe strongly in a dog-friendly work environment, let everybody know about it. At least that way you won't make the mistake of hiring someone who's allergic to dogs, or worse, a cat person!

TRUST ME, THE GRASS ISN'T ANY GREENER

In the early days of my business, I remember looking at enterprise-level companies and thinking, "Wow, they must have flawless operations and run so fucking smoothly. I can't wait until we get there."

Sadly, after diving pretty deeply into researching and physically visiting those companies and how they operate, I realized something a little surprising, which was "They're just as fucked up and batshit crazy as we are!" It's true; the size of the company and the strength of the product or service doesn't matter when it comes to operating a business. No matter how big you are, how great your product is, and how well you communicate, things get fucked up! In fact, after I really started to investigate some of those companies, I realized they might be even crazier than we are.

GOING FOR PASSION

Teams are like families in a lot of ways. They challenge, bicker, and insult each other on occasion. I've even seen a fistfight or two break out. That usually means the two combatants care enough about the outcome to actually want to punch each other in the face for what they believe in. To be clear, I'm not suggesting such a reaction is appropriate, but when something like that happens, at least you know the passion is there. It might be misplaced, but it's there.

With passion at the heart of the corporate dynamic, great teams can push the boundaries of what seems attainable. Individuals become ten times stronger—physically and mentally—to do things they never thought they were capable of. Not only do I support this mentality, but I embody it. I want people to push me out of my comfort zone just as hard as I try to push them. It's the only way to sustain real growth and is central to the concept of the graduating mindset. That's why, when my friend Brandon texted me, "Hey, do you want to climb Mount Rainier with us?" a few years ago, without hesitation I said, "Hell yeah!"

The timing was perfect. Brandon sent me that text precisely when I was in search of my next epic life experience. Every so often, if somebody doesn't push me to do something crazy, I push myself. In this case, Brandon stepped up and gave me a push like a wild, stampeding elephant.

RAINIER: A TALL TESTAMENT TO TEAMWORK

If you know anything about mountain climbing, you know that Mount Rainier is not something an out-of-shape, untrained, inexperienced person should ever attempt. Mount Rainier is 14,411 feet above sea level and the highest mountain in the Pacific Northwest. Typically, it requires strict training regimens of six to eight months for most experienced mountain climbers. Some people train for years just to get to base camp. I, however, spent two weeks watching a bunch of mountain-climbing videos on YouTube while logging some serious miles on my stairclimber. If you're thinking, "What a dumb ass!" you're not alone.

I talked to several experienced mountain climbers during those two weeks, and every one of them told me that I wasn't going to make it. In fact, most of them told me that I was a fool for even attempting it. Even the people I leaned on for support, like my girlfriend at the time, told me I was an idiot. I don't think I talked to one sober person who thought I was going to make it to the top of that fucking mountain. Of course, that made me want to do it even more.

It goes to show that people can push you in different ways. They can motivate you by saying, "Sure you can climb Mount Rainier with only two weeks of training, Ben. Why not throw in a triathlon and an arm-wrestling match with Hulk Hogan when you get to the summit?" Or they can motivate you by saying, "You are such a dipshit. What makes you think you're going to climb one of the biggest mountains in the country? Have fun dying, jackass!"

I have to admit, after I put on that fifty-pound backpack and my body was operating at about half its normal oxygen supply, I started to agree with the haters. I began to wonder what the fuck I was thinking. About forty-five minutes into the climb and approximately one-hundredth of the way there, my body was hurting more than it ever had before. Given the choice of that Malagasy prison or this, I would have happily huddled in the fetal position on that interrogation room floor without a second thought.

WE'RE NOT EVEN CLOSE

That was my moment of doubt. My feet stopped moving and, for a split second, I thought, "Nope, this isn't going to happen. I'm either going to just sit here for a couple of hours and walk back when I'm ready, or I'll stay at base camp once we get there." Right as those thoughts were settling in and I was dreaming of blankets, open fires, and hot cocoa, Brandon's voice broke through the serenity with, "Fuck you, pussy! We're not even close to base camp. Get your fat ass moving!"

Summitting Mt. Rainier, Washington (We're not even close!)

Pretty much every time I slowed down, Brandon fucked with me in that way. Some would see that as being motivating; others may interpret it as being a douche. To this day, I'm not really sure which perspective I agree with more. Once again, it's all about perspective. The point is that he kept me moving. That's what great teams do, and this team, which consisted of Brandon, me, and another one of Brandon's Air Force pilot buddies named Colby, was a legendary one.

Brandon taught me how to use a mountain-climbing technique called a rest step. It allowed me to use about half the energy of a full step. That might seem like a small thing, but I was exhausted almost before we began, so that little piece of advice probably saved my ass.

At one point, I told Brandon and Colby to cruise ahead and I would meet them at base camp in another hour and a half or so. Colby went ahead, but Brandon stuck with me until we got about thirty minutes away from base camp. That's when he forged ahead to help get things set up.

Maybe fifteen minutes after he left, a massive snowstorm was coming directly toward me. Picture how hard it is to drive a car in a blizzard, except take away the heater, add a fifty-pound sack to your back, and understand that if you misstep, you'll likely fall down a giant crevasse to your imminent death.

As the prologue of that storm was pelting me in the face with tiny flakes of snow and balls of ice, I kept thinking that I needed to pick up the pace or I was going to die before I got to base camp. Worse than death, I was going to look like a little bitch in front of my buddies. With those thoughts circling in my half-frostbitten brain, I pushed harder and harder, until I made it to camp just before the heart of that storm hit.

BASE CAMP

When we finished getting the tents set up, we made a plan to leave for the summit at 1:00 a.m. That meant we would get about three hours of sleep before moving forward. After considering how slow I was, however, Brandon and Colby decided we should leave around midnight, giving us a total of around two hours of sleep between the already exhausting climb to base camp and the next ten hours of summiting.

I'm not sure if any of us slept more than an hour that night. It was too fucking cold for one thing, and for another, my body was in the most severe agony it had ever experienced in my entire life. As my muscles were throbbing and my skin was freezing, my mind began revisiting my options.

For another split second, I thought about staying at base camp, giving Brandon and Colby the middle finger when they tried to get me moving again, and going blissfully back to sleep for the next sixteen hours, if I didn't freeze first. The other idea was to just start walking back and get the hell out of there. Admittedly, both options seemed appealing at first, but then I had the come-to-Jesus moment I needed.

I said to myself, "Ben, you could legitimately die somewhere on the side of that mountain tonight. This is no joke, asshole. Your body is completely fucked right now and you're not even one-fifth of the way to the top. I know you have a big ego and feel like you have to prove something to yourself all the time, but this is serious shit. Is this singular challenge really worth risking your life over? This random thing that you didn't even bother to seriously train for—is it worth it?"

That's when I realized it wasn't about that one thing. The mountain was just a metaphor. I'd said I was going to do it. If I gave up at base camp, what else would I give up on that I had committed to doing?

At some point throughout that evening, probably in a half-conscious state between dreaming and death, I came to terms with what I was going to do. I accepted that I could possibly die while trying to climb that mountain, but at least then I wouldn't have to be pissed at myself for quitting.

Somehow, the rest of that night was a little more peaceful

after I'd determined that I really had no other choice. I was going to get to the summit or die trying.

SUMMIT OR DIE

"Guys," I said, "I'm going to do this. I'm going to summit this mountain." We packed as lightly as possible before leaving base camp and started hiking toward the summit of Mount Rainier. Brandon responded to my optimism with his usual smart-ass mantra: "Good for you, but we're not even close."

"What a dick!" I said under my breath.

The next sixteen hours were the hardest of my life, but I soldiered on while taking one step at a time. Walking over fourteen thousand feet on flat land during a blizzard would have been hard enough, but adding some legit elevation to that pushed my boundaries far past anything I'd ever imagined physically and mentally possible.

My face was blasted continuously with snow and ice. I was hot and cold at the same time, because although we were getting hit by a blizzard, we were also marching much closer to the sun. Not only was my body all fucked up from fatigue, but it was also weakening from a cold sweat.

After a few hours, I thought to myself, "There's no way

I'm going to make it. I'm going to die here." It didn't help that Brandon was reminding me the whole time, "Dude, we're not even close." That little fucker said that until we were about thirty seconds away from the summit.

Another challenge throughout the climb—one that could have easily killed any of us—were these cracks in the ice of the glacier that formed crevasses anywhere from two hundred to five hundred feet deep. We had to get a running start and jump over each one of them. There were about five or six of them, and they each represented one scary-as-hell moment. One false move—a slip, trip, or mistimed jump—and the climb would be over. In fact, that's exactly what had happened to someone earlier that day.

Apparently, someone had tried to go super fast down the mountain and had fallen into one of those crevasses and died. We found out about it later that day, so we actually jumped over his dead body on our way up the mountain—calming, I know.

Throughout the first leg of the climb after we stopped at base camp, we saw some hikers turn around and head back. They told us that some rockslides were occurring in that same area. Turns out there were a few extra people on the mountain and that had caused some rocks to get kicked down, which was not conducive to a safe climb.

I talked to a few different people on their way back down. Most of them told me they had been training for years to make the trip. It was incredibly sad to me that these people had given up on a dream because, either physically or mentally, they had reached their limits. I remember thinking to myself how difficult it was going to be for them to live with that afterward.

The idea that some people who had trained so hard and so long for that day were turning around began seriously fucking with my mental state. I had only been training for a couple of weeks, and I had already accepted the fact that I could die. But now I was beginning to consider death as more and more of a possibility.

I never expressed any of those thoughts aloud, but once in a while I asked, "Are we there yet?" like an eight-year-old on a long car ride in the back seat of his parents' SUV. Brandon never disappointed me with his response. Predictably, he answered as he had been doing all along: "Dude, we're not even close." It was like a stab in the heart every time he said it, and the further we got, the more I wanted to choke him for it.

Eventually, we got to a major marking point that meant we were about a half-hour from the summit. That's where we dropped some gear off to shed a little weight and took a short break to sit down. I was told not to fall asleep because at that altitude you risk taking what they call a *snow nap*, which is essentially a nap you don't wake up from because your body gets so depleted of oxygen.

After we agreed that we had rested enough, we looked at each other and said, "Let's fucking do this." Then, we began the homestretch of our climb.

Around three minutes before we reached the summit, it hit me, "Holy shit, we're actually going to get to the top of Mount Rainier."

I'm not a big cry-guy and I don't generally like to admit the rare occasion that brings me to tears, but when we approached the summit, I couldn't hold it in any longer.

I felt a unique mixture of emotions. There was accomplishment, exhaustion, and jubilation that resulted in this odd half-cry, half-laugh burst of audible energy. A sense of inner pride came over me that I had pushed my physical and mental capacity further than I'd dreamed possible. It was an incredible feat, but it never would have happened without the construction of that superstar team.

ALL FOR ONE AND ONE FOR ALL

We all supported each other the whole way. Although I

desperately wanted to strangle Brandon every time he gave me his, "We're not even close." mantra, I knew he was only motivating me in his own weird way.

Without an extremely high level of teamwork, we could have never made it to the summit. Our hands were so cold that we had to help each other do everything. We boiled water together, fed each other, and formed an incredible bond that will never be broken. It was a no-man-left-behind mission. If one of us died along the way, we would have dragged the dead body up to the summit and back down the mountain.

Trust and loyalty were taken to new levels on that mission. Failure was not an option, and we pushed each other to our absolute limits to achieve our goal.

Key Takeaway #11: Whether you're climbing a mountain or running a business, if you have that same high level of teamwork, success is inevitable. If everybody is pushing toward the same end goal and willing to die for it, your true boundaries are much further than you have ever dreamed possible.

Summit of Mt. Rainier (Smiles all around, until ... we realized we then had to climb back down.)

Chapter Nine

DISCONNECT TO RECONNECT

The greatest threat to our planet is to believe that someone else will save it.

—ROBERT SWAN (WORLD-RENOWNED EXPLORER, AUTHOR)

As far as I know, there is no emoji to describe the feeling of getting to the summit of Mount Rainier. It's a feeling unlike any other I've ever experienced, even with all my travels and adventures around the world. Actually, I'm not sure if there's one for navigating a death-defying turn at Gorman Canyon or ending up in a Malagasy prison interrogation room, either.

Those are all experiences you can't get from a smartphone, tablet, or laptop. You have to be present in your life to appreciate the beauty, fear, and excitement of them. As a society, I feel like we've all become too connected to these devices we carry with us at all times. Most of us are too busy waiting for our next text, notification, or social media alert to truly appreciate the thrill of the present moment.

Not every moment is filled with extreme accomplishment or happiness, but each one can be beautiful in its own way. How would you feel if you missed your child's first steps because you were sending a text? Shooting stars can be an awesome sight, but you'll never know it if you're too busy looking at your phone to ever gaze at the dark blue beauty of a clear, early evening sky. More importantly, what if I had been inexplicably playing Candy Crush on my iPhone in that Malagasy prison when our planting partner Josy walked by that window? You wouldn't be reading this book, and I would probably be holed up in unspeakable living conditions with fifteen other dudes, sharing a five-by-five room with one toilet and two disgusting soiled mattresses. Dare I mention the rats and bugs that would be competing for those mattresses? Or, if I were lucky, I'd be dead.

I always knew that there was more to life than constant electronic interaction, but it never became more obvious to me than during my recent expedition to Antarctica.

A CONTINENTAL SHIFT IN MINDSET

A lot of people can say they've been to six continents. Six is easy. There's at least one location on all six of them that is unbelievably fun to experience and has nonstop flights arriving and departing all day and night.

That seventh continent—Antarctica—is the tough one to get to. It's our southernmost continent and is considered the world's largest desert because of its lack of precipitation. It's also the one continent I hadn't visited until recently, when world-renowned explorer Robert Swan invited me to join him on a monthlong expedition.

Rob Swan and Ben discussing global planting strategy, Antarctica (Yes, Rob actually uses those goggles.)

"Holy shit!" were the first two words that came out of my mouth when Robert invited me on an expedition to Antarctica with him. "Fuck yes!" were the next two words. Robert told me that he loved my company's mission to plant trees all over the world, and he wanted me to come to Antarctica with him to experience the serenity and beauty of the seventh continent and also work with his team of researchers and scientists on ideas and implement ways to *save the Antarctic*.

Antarctica has to be seen to be believed. When we arrived, I felt like I was in a mythical land. I saw penguins waddling all around us, massive glaciers sticking up around our ship like New York City skyscrapers, and seals lying on their sides with their heads raised, staring at us, almost as if to say, "What the fuck are you guys doing here?"

The snow was pure white. I know what you're thinking. "D'uh Ben, snow is *definitely* white." This was a different kind of white; it was almost blinding in its purity. I sat in the snow and saw giant glaciers floating in the ominous-looking blue waters. My mouth and my eyes were wide open as I tried to take in the unequivocal serenity of the moment. Needless to say, my smartphone was the furthest thing from my mind.

Selfie with Penguin (I mean, the caption says it all; It's a selfie with a penguin!)

BEING HUMAN

After the first four to five days of the trip, I noticed that I felt incredibly close to all the people who were on the trip with me. It was a strange feeling because we'd known each other for such a short time, but I felt as if they'd already become some of my best friends. In fact, I felt like I knew them on a deeper level than some of my friends back home.

As I was journaling about my experience with these

people, I had an epiphany. The reason we had become so close was that there was nothing to distract us. In case you're wondering, cell reception is absolutely nonexistent, so there was no checking in to the South Pole on Facebook. Even satellite phone reception for the most part is unusable.

Instead of gazing intently at the warm glow of an iPhone, we were sitting down to have meals together and talking. We didn't just talk about the expedition. I had recently been through a big relationship change, but I felt surprisingly comfortable talking about it in detail with these people. At the same time, two or three other people opened up about their personal lives as well. Before long, we were sharing this vulnerability and an openness that was so refreshingly honest. We had conversations with each other that you typically have with a best friend of over ten years.

"Holy shit!" I thought. "What if all of our relationships as a society were this open and free from distraction? If a group of strangers could establish a strong bond in two weeks, what sorts of conversations and connectedness would be possible if we untethered ourselves from our smartphones and tablets?"

Our society has become so overstimulated with constant electronic interaction that most of us have forgotten how to have meaningful dialogue with each other. People barely even call each other anymore. Instead we text with acronyms like LMAO, LMK, YOLO, TTYL, or DILLIGAS (do I look like I give a shit). I haven't seen that last one used too often, but it's out there and kind of funny, so I thought I'd mention it. Text acronyms are symbolic of how poor our communication with each other has become. They mean we don't have enough time for each other anymore to use real words.

My experience on this trip drove me to consider shutting down all my social media accounts and going all-out caveman on the world. If I'd stayed in Antarctica long enough, I might have abandoned electricity and indoor plumbing, too, but probably not.

BALANCE

After multiple journal entries that explored this revelation, I ultimately decided that balance was the key to maintaining positive human interaction in the Technological Age.

I built my business through technology, so for me to bash all electronics all the time would be hypocritical. A certain amount of digital interaction is necessary in modern society. As I examined the value of technology as deeply as I could, I also realized that I can use technology to create more good. By spreading the word of planting trees and preaching the values of a socially conscious business model through social media, I can reach a hell of a lot more people than I could have in the pre-internet age.

By balancing technology with real human interaction, I can get the best out of both worlds. I didn't close down my social media accounts, nor did I throw my iPhone into a recycling bin. Instead, I set my phone to receive zero notifications other than phone calls. That way, nothing else takes me away from the present moment. The odds of an interruption happening to a meaningful conversation I'm engaged in are greatly diminished. No longer am I constantly beeped or buzzed to disengage from the present moment.

As I'm writing this, it's been about ten months since I arrived home from Antarctica and implemented a more sensible balance between technology and humanity. I can already feel how much closer my relationships have been. Conversations with friends, family members, and coworkers are much more productive and meaningful than ever before. I can look people in the eyes, talk to them, and listen more intently.

I'm only twenty-eight, so most of my adult life has been spent using technology all day, every day. That means I have difficulty with the idea of balance. I'm so preconditioned to use electronics in abundance that even with a strong determination to disconnect in order to reconnect, I still struggle mightily at times. I've become more adept at ignoring texts and notifications, but I still check emails a little too often. It's a work in progress, but I think the end goal is worth the fight.

Key Takeaway #12: Especially when starting your business, you need to create some headspace, some time to disconnect and reset. Doing this, perhaps on a weekly basis, will better enable you to fully show up for your business and your employees.

Disconnecting to reconnect has proven invaluable to me. Without it, my company wouldn't exist, this book wouldn't have been written, and my brain and body would be fried.

THE ELEVATOR CHALLENGE

Are you up for the idea of disconnecting to reconnect? If not, just skip to the next section. No hard feelings, I promise. If you're game, however, keep reading because I've got a little challenge for you.

Prepare yourself—young Jedi of attempted disconnectedness—for the Elevator Challenge:

The next time you're in a crowded elevator—one with

five or more people in it—look around you. I guarantee that about 90 percent of those people will be looking at their phones. Here's the best part about this: an elevator is basically a metal cage that ascends and descends between walls made of thick metal. Unless it's some sort of magical elevator, no cell signals can penetrate that box, because it's essentially a giant Faraday cage. That means people are staring at their phones for no damned good reason.

If you really pay attention the next time you're in a crowded elevator, you'll see what I mean. People will open up their phones and just scroll from screen to screen with no particular purpose; there can't be, because there is no fucking service!

Why the fuck does everybody stare at their phones in an elevator when the phones clearly are not working? The answer is simple: they want to avoid human contact. Most people in today's eternal electronic environment would rather stare at a glowing screen that does absolutely nothing than initiate an actual conversation with a fellow human being.

The next time you're in such a situation, my challenge to you is to break the silence and give someone in the elevator a compliment. Don't be weird about it or gross in any way. Just tell somebody, "Hey, cool shoes, dude," or, "Hey, love that shirt."

The world needs your fucking ideas, but the world also needs better fucking human interaction. Don't be afraid to help a friend in need or give a stranger a compliment. Maybe you have an idea to help people interact with each other better. Maybe you have an idea to help people become more mindful and live in the present moment more often. Maybe you have an idea to create a globally impactful volunteer organization. We all have the power to make this world a better place, but we have to go from idea to execution at some point, and the time is now. This is the reason I knew I absolutely had to write this book.

AHA AT YOGA

A healthy balance of technology and humanity goes further than turning off cell notifications. There are activities that foster a more mindful presence, such as working out, meditation, and yoga. Pick one that works for you and dedicate yourself to it.

I regularly attend a one-hour yoga class, to help me in my quest for balance, where I shut off my phone and enjoy exercising in the present moment. During one of my sessions I had an aha moment. I realized that I was doing too much in my business. Everything from operations to sales and production had my name all over it, and that had to change.

Although the company was thriving, it occurred to me

that the situation was going to hit a point of critical mass eventually, because I wasn't allowing people to develop. By doing everything on my own, I was inadvertently stunting their career growth and placing a serious limitation on the viable longevity of the business.

As soon as I got back from the yoga class, I made a plan that night to let some aspects of the business go to other capable, loyal people whom I trusted completely.

The next morning, I hired someone to be the president of the company and communicated to the entire team that I was planning to step back and let them take their careers and the company to the next level. I was going to focus exclusively on high-level issues like acquisition, public speaking engagements, and writing this book.

So far, the results of that empowerment have been extremely promising. As such, I'm eternally grateful for that aha moment. It's proof that you don't need to go to Antarctica for inspiration. It's all around you. Inspiration could occur during a one-hour yoga class just as easily as a two-month journey to the South Pole, but you have to be focused enough for the idea to develop. If you're too busy keeping up with a constant barrage of texts and social media buzz, the idea may never fully form, and not only will you be missing out, but so will the rest of the world.

Chapter Ten

I HOPE YOU LIKE YOURSELF

A journey of a thousand miles starts with a single step.
—LAO TZU (CHINESE PHILOSOPHER AND WRITER)

I get the impression that some people think of entrepreneurship as a super-networking lifestyle, where you're always making powerful connections and everybody wants to know you and be with you. That is absolutely not the case. Being a business owner isn't always as glorious as conquering Mount Rainier with a superstar team, or as inspiring as a journey to Antarctica with a world-famous explorer. The truth is that it can be a deep, dark, lonely fucking road to travel sometimes. You have to ask yourself if you're ready for that.

I'LL SLEEP WHEN I'M DEAD

As you can imagine, money was tight in the early days of my business. Dinner on a lot of nights for me was canned green beans and tuna fish, and we had to cut a lot of corners in our operation's expenses. I remember one time when we had some legal documents that needed to be reviewed, but we couldn't afford a lawyer. There had to be hundreds of pages to read through and sign. Guess what happens when you're a business owner and you can't afford to pay someone to do that sort of thing? You do it.

I locked myself in a room and didn't sleep for three days. How glorious is that? Those are the types of moments that are incredibly lonely and all too frequent at every stage of a business. I had no choice in the matter because nobody else was going to do it. We needed to sign those legal documents to successfully enable a launch with our first distributor in over five hundred bookstores.

It wasn't just a matter of signing on the dotted line. I needed to understand what those documents actually meant. Remember what happened when I thought we had sold a bazillion units in Target and Best Buy? If I hadn't been such a dumbass, I would have realized that we were selling those things on consignment, and I could have avoided the deep, dark, lonely place of facing the high likelihood of catastrophic failure.

I think I missed a friend's wedding the weekend I spent poring over all that legal mumbo jumbo, but I had no choice. It was a lonely, sleep-deprived, shitty experience, but I had to do it if my business was going to get to the next level. Once again, I needed to remember *why* I was doing that. If it was purely about making money, I probably would have shredded everything, gone to my friend's wedding, and had a kick-ass time instead.

Well, it's not like that anymore, though, right?

Actually, it is. Since then, I've had probably a hundred or more similar thrill rides. In fact, right now I could be out downhill mountain biking with a friend. Instead, I'm writing this book because it means a lot to me, and it's a piece of my mission to change this planet. It must mean a lot to me, because I fucking love downhill mountain biking!

Much like I told myself that I was going to climb Mount Rainier, I also told myself that I was going to write this book, so that's all that had to be said in my mind. It's much less about the ability to do something, and more about making the commitment to do it. However, I'm stoked to think about the possibilities for its release, so it's not nearly as bad as poring over hundreds of pages of legal chaos. Of course, it's not as exciting as downhill mountain biking, either, but very little is, in my opinion.

That's life as a business owner. Whenever a situation arises that nobody else will take care of, you're the last person standing, and the more your business grows, the lonelier it will get.

My experience with Mount Rainier serves as an effective metaphor here as well. There were a lot less climbers at the top of that mountain than there were at the base. It's the same way in business. The more your business grows, the more people you'll meet who want to be with you just for the money. In the early days, there may be only a few occasions that require all-nighters, but as your business reaches higher levels, you will have smaller circles of trust-based friends you can truly talk about anything with.

THE BREAKUP

I've grown to accept a certain level of solitude as part of the entrepreneurial journey. I've never felt more alone or emotionally vulnerable, however, than I did on a trip to Saudi Arabia a few years ago.

That trip occurred during an extremely troubling time in my personal life. I had been dating someone for about two years, had bought a ring, and was ready to get married. I felt like I already knew where our life together was heading. Then, like a sucker punch from an unknown assailant, we split up. Thinking about the disintegration of all the plans we'd made absolutely crushed me. I became despondent and didn't know where to turn.

The breakup put me in a completely fucked-up mindset. But I'm not the type to sit still and wallow in anything for too long. I try to stay generally positive. There are way too many incredible things to do and amazing places to see in this world to spend too much time in such an unproductive manner. Nonetheless, sadness and negativity overwhelmed me for some length of time, and I became mentally shut down. I had invested so much time and energy in that relationship, and I had assumed it would work out the same way my business had, but it didn't. The toughest idea to accept was that I had put 110 percent of my effort into this, and that wasn't enough. So, therefore, I thought I was not enough.

EMBRACE YOUR VULNERABILITIES

Part of human nature is to put on this mask of invincibility and pretend nothing bothers us. Well, that's bullshit, if you ask me. I dismiss any book from a business leader who makes it sound like they've never struggled with relationships, business decisions, or anything else. That's a fairy tale, not a real book with real lessons and real value.

I've made a special effort in this book to talk about some of the things I've struggled so intensely with in my life and in my business. For example, I failed when I sold those cases to the big-box stores in the early going. No excuses, just failure, and it put me in a bad place for a while. Guess what? I'm okay with that.

I was probably a little foolish when I assumed Trish was just going to hand money to Kevin and me without any repercussions later. That's okay, too, because I learned a lot from that experience.

And when this relationship ended, I was devastated. Why? Because I'm human and pain hurts, whether it's emotional or physical in nature.

Those things don't portray weakness in my opinion, however; they show my humanity. By exposing our vulnerabilities—as humans—we become stronger, not weaker. Once you accept and embrace your vulnerabilities as a human, nobody can stop you from reaching higher and higher. David Goggins speaks remarkably well to this notion in his epic, true-life story, *Can't Hurt Me*. Check it out if you need some inspirational advice or just a quick reminder that embracing the vulnerability of our humanity makes us stronger than ever.

A SANDY SITUATION

While attempting to come to terms with the dissolution

of that relationship, I decided to go on a trip to Saudi Arabia with my good friend Nanxi and two other entrepreneurs. It was an attempt to break my routine, get away, and do some soul-searching—because there's no better place to go for a relaxing mental retreat than an unstable Middle Eastern country that requires a waiver from the US government, a "reason for travel" application from the Saudi government, and a Saudi diplomat to sign off on the travel.

The opportunity for soul-searching hit me in the face pretty hard one day. I decided to rent a big sand truck and check out some sand dunes that were about three hours away from where we were staying. It sounded like a harmless enough thing to do—if I had been in the United States and there had been a city nearby—but that wasn't the case.

Those sand dunes were far away from civilization, had the purest sand, and were an incredible sight. There was nothing but rolling sand dunes in sight as I tore through, up, and over these incredible land masses. After cruising around some massive sand dunes for about thirty minutes, my tires began to lose traction. I must have hit a hot patch; my tires sank a bit to where the sand wasn't nearly as firm. I tried to stay calm, but I also knew I had driven to the middle of nowhere. This wasn't an area where cars routinely drove by, so if I was stuck, I could have been stuck for an awfully long time.

Being a big fan of four-wheelers, I thought that truck might have had a sand setting on it, and it did. Calm, cool, and collected, I hit the sand setting, which essentially lets some pressure out of the tires and allows it to get out of almost any situation like this one. Unfortunately, this was one of the rare occasions where the sand setting did not work.

Weatherwise, it was a fairly typical day in Saudi Arabia, which meant it was around one hundred degrees Fahrenheit, not exactly ideal for a ten- to twelve-hour walk back to civilization. I was trying to figure out if I was going to risk sunstroke and plain old *stroke* to brave such a hike in the desert or wait by the truck, just in case some other moron decided to come out here like I had.

At that moment, I remembered something my cousin Mike used to say a lot: "Life's a rocky road. Good thing we have big tires." I had to laugh out loud like a lunatic when I thought of those words. Mentally, I was stuck because the tires of my emotional state weren't big enough to get out of the hole left by a shattered relationship. Physically, I was stuck because the actual tires of the piece of shit truck I'd rented weren't big enough to get out of the holes they'd dug in the sand.

I decided to stay with the truck for a while. The thought of a ten-hour hike in the hot-as-hell Saudi Arabian desert was about as appealing as attempting that climb up Mount Rainier stark naked. All I needed to enhance the experience would have been Brandon busting my balls the whole time: "Dude, we're not even close."

Middle of Bumfuck Nowhere Sand Dunes, Saudi Arabia (Pre-militant guys (not shown) helping me get unstuck)

THE POWER OF JOURNALING

That's when I took out my journal and started writing. I wrote for about a half hour, and it made me feel a lot better about my current personal situation. Getting all my emotional baggage out on paper has always been such a cathartic experience for me, and this time was no different.

Then I started flipping through previous pages to look at some old entries from a couple of years back. I began to notice some commonalities between the older entries and my most recent writings. The situations were different, but I used a lot of the same words to describe my feelings. What I couldn't get over, however, was that my mindset had graduated by about ten levels since I'd written those older journal entries, yet I was experiencing the same emotional difficulties over a relationship gone bad.

A deeper exploration of those older entries revealed that my graduating mindset always found a way to pick me up from whatever personal struggle I was facing. I achieved a tremendous peace of mind that day, sitting on the hood of that stuck truck and realizing that I had the mental capacity to rise above anything. It didn't matter if it was tens of thousands of unsold units, a pending lawsuit for $1.5 million, being held against my will in a Malagasy prison, or being stuck in some stupid fucking sand dunes in the Middle East. A great calmness washed over my sun-blistered face as I read those pages, and I knew I was going to get out of that shithole one way or another.

About forty-five minutes later, I thought I saw a jeep in the distance. I remembered all those old movies where people got stuck in the desert and began to hallucinate. I was desperately hoping that I wasn't seeing a mirage, but I also thought that maybe the dudes in that jeep weren't going to be so friendly, so it might be better if they were a mirage.

Sure enough, they were no mirage. A jeep pulled up alongside the shitty truck I rented and some guys got out to investigate the situation. At first, they didn't seem overly friendly and started yelling something I couldn't understand. Then they started waving their hands around like they were getting pissed off. "Not good," I thought to myself. "There's no way I'm going to get out of a second prison overseas as easily as I did the first one. If these guys decide to fuck with me, there's not a damned thing I can do about it. I don't even have Roger with me this time."

I kept pointing at my tires and screaming, "They're under sand! I'm stuck!" as if saying something louder somehow makes it more understandable to a person speaking a foreign language (typical American move).

For some reason I still don't know, all of a sudden they stopped yelling, put their hands down, and pulled some straps out of their vehicle to help pull me out of the sand. I have no idea what changed their temperament, but they turned out to be good dudes. I didn't have to improvise my way out of a foreign jail and all was right in the world once again.

I gave those guys some cash for helping me and was able to drive back a few miles to the main road to eventually get back to the city. When I got there, I was in a much better place mentally than I'd been when I left. My journaling experience had shifted my mindset. I had graduated it once again.

Journaling has always been a big part of my life. It's helped me to internally work out a lot of situations along my entrepreneurial journey. By getting my thoughts down on paper and being able to refer to them at a later date as a refresher, I get so much value. It's a great way to sort out a lot of emotional baggage and grow as an individual and as a businessperson. That's a big reason why we sell so many journal notebooks at WOODCHUCK. They're meant to be taken back into nature and to help people get in touch with their innermost thoughts and feelings.

Outside of my practicing faith and learning from my incredible mentors, journaling is the most productive thing I do to graduate my mindset and evolve as a person and an entrepreneur. It helps me to stay on track with who I want to become. Journaling is also effective for getting ideas out as a stream of consciousness. Lastly, it's a great coping mechanism for those days when you're feeling lonely at the top.

Key Takeaway #13: If there's one thing that you take from this book (well, I hope there's more than one thing you take from it), make journaling an active part of your day, week, or month. Shameless plug: of course, it's even better if you buy a WOODCHUCK journal and use it outside, in nature.

There is no greater power than being alone with your thoughts and working them out on a physical piece of paper (ideally somewhere in nature) to cure something that's currently troubling or challenging you. Journaling in this way has the ability to launch you on a trajectory toward your dream future and millions of miles past what you ever dreamed possible.

Chapter Eleven

GREAT LEADERS KNOW WHEN TO LEAD AND WHEN TO EMPOWER

Empowerment isn't a buzzword among leadership gurus. It's a proven technique where leaders give their teams the appropriate training, tools, resources, and guidance to succeed.

—JOHN RAMPTON (AMERICAN ENTREPRENEUR AND STARTUP ENTHUSIAST)

Leadership is about so much more than simply barking orders at people and expecting them to do a great job. There are times, like in the previous chapter, when you have to step up because nobody else knows what to do. There are other occasions when you need to empower others by preparing them with the required tools and knowledge. Empowerment is a bit of an art form. You need to trust the people you're delegating authority to.

Knowing when to lead and when to empower is a difficult question. The answer might be different for everybody. For me, it's mostly a gut feeling. The longer I've been in business, the stronger my gut has gotten for making a good choice between when to empower and when to lead. I usually weigh the pros of giving a trusted employee an opportunity to grow their skillset versus the potential consequences of failure.

Key Takeaway #14: Many situations call for a balance between leadership and empowerment. This occurs when the situation is too demanding for any one person—even the business owner—to get the job done. When this happens, you need to get your hands dirty and work with the team.

Boss vs. Leader (I mean don't get me wrong, the boss does look pretty comfortable.)

In that case, you're still the leader calling the shots, but you're also on the ground floor producing alongside everybody else. At the same time, you're empowering others to ensure they're doing their part to the best of their abilities. In the end, you hope the collective efforts of an empowered team with focused leadership meets the end goal. When that happens, celebrate the achievement together and ensure that everyone knows how important they were to the successful completion of the task.

In the first year or two of WOODCHUCK's existence, we had a situation that required a delicate balance of leadership and empowerment. The task at hand required a total team effort and someone to make the right decisions.

We had to fill a large order in a condensed time frame for something we had never done before.

HOW MANY WOODEN WINE BOXES COULD A WOODCHUCK CHUCK IF A WOODCHUCK COULD CHUCK WOODEN WINE BOXES?

Chipotle ordered twelve thousand wooden wine boxes from WOODCHUCK, a huge order for a young, growing business. However, we had some serious logistical problems to overcome that made filling that order quite challenging:

- We had never made wine boxes before.
- They needed the entire order completed and shipped within one week.
- WOODCHUCK had about ten employees to produce the entire order with none of the equipment needed to make wooden wine boxes.
- We had to figure out how to personally deliver the shipment one thousand miles away.

Everything else was just fucking perfect!

Right away, I knew the entire company had to go into *beast mode*. We needed all hands on deck. Everybody had to be pushing in the same direction toward a unified goal of getting twelve thousand units built, loaded, and delivered in less than seven days. We also needed someone at the front of the line showing people what to do and how to do it—leadership by example. That job was mine. It wasn't as simple as barking orders at everyone. I had to get my hands dirty and work my ass off like everyone else.

Our corporate culture of supporting creativity and innovation came through in a big way in that situation. Somebody had the idea to build a machine that shot two nails into the sides of the boxes, which allowed us to build one box every fifteen seconds. That was a monumental contribution to the task.

Somehow, we got everything built with a day to spare. At that point, the only remaining problem was getting them shipped to Colorado in time. The day before the order was due, I purchased a twenty-five-foot trailer, which we loaded that night and drove to Chipotle's warehouse. It was another sleepless night, because there was no time for rest. There was a lot of money at stake and the business's survival was dependent on meeting the deadline, so sleep would have to wait.

When we arrived in Colorado, we were pretty beat up from our labors and lack of sleep, but we helped the Chipotle employees unload the boxes and assisted in filling the boxes with the wine and packaging materials. As a young, hungry business, those are the types of things you do to rise above the competition, rested or not.

The quality of our product, timeliness of the delivery, and extra service at the finish line blew Chipotle away. They were extremely impressed by our overall operations, and I was ecstatic about the way my team came together to help the company survive and grow.

None of it would have happened if I hadn't had the right people who understood the *why* of my business, pushing toward the same goal and supporting each other the whole way. It was also crucial that, as a leader, I understood how my team needed me.

Total empowerment wasn't the right choice because we had never made wine boxes before, so nobody knew where to start. Authoritarian leadership, however, wasn't correct either, because we needed all hands on deck. If I had stood up in an ivory tower somewhere and bellowed orders through an intercom, nobody would have been inspired enough to create that hugely impactful machine that drove nails into the boxes. Beyond that, nobody would have even given half a shit if we'd gotten the job done, because they would have felt too disconnected from the leadership. They likely would have loathed the leadership, which is never an ideal scenario.

IT'S OKAY TO LET OTHERS FAIL

Things aren't always going to work out as well as they did

for us in that Chipotle example. In that situation, it was essential for my team to see me get my hands dirty and join them in production efforts. That experience had a positive effect on other managers at my company, too, and they followed suit with my approach to leadership by example.

In other situations, however, a different approach might be necessary, even if it means letting someone fail. For example, we had a salesperson who had some decision-making responsibilities about a year ago. He had an idea to invest over $30,000 on a celebrity gifting suite.

On the surface, that might have sounded like a fine idea, but I knew we had tried it multiple times in the past and it never worked. I told him that, but it didn't change his mind. He was certain that this time would be different. He thought he knew how to make it work and was convinced it would succeed if I let him do it.

I thought about it for a while. There was no way his idea was going to work, but I also knew that $30,000 wasn't going to break the bank, so I told him, "Go for it! But I want you to track everything you're doing so we can replicate it when it succeeds."

Ultimately, I decided it was worth the monetary loss to build a good relationship with this individual. I could have told him, "No, your idea fucking blows. Get the hell out of here now and think of something else." But what would that have accomplished? Certainly not any level of confidence or support. There's also no lesson involved in that.

By empowering him to make his own decision, which was part of his job anyway, I showed him that I trusted his decision-making ability and valued his opinion. It also set the stage for similar situations that will arise in the future, because we'll have established a collaborative rapport.

In the end, his idea crashed and burned just as hard as I thought it would. I could have greeted him with a big fat "I fucking told you so," but that wouldn't have accomplished anything. Nothing more needed to be said. He knew it didn't work out. He also knew I'd cautioned him against it. But because of his true confidence to execute his plan differently than others before him, he thought the outcome would be different.

If I had implemented authoritarian leadership and just overruled him in the first place, he wouldn't have learned anything. Now he knows the value of considering other opinions just as highly as his own, and he'll be able to make better choices using more collaboration in his decision-making process. These are valuable lessons for him to take forward.

Losing money sucks, so I understand that it's hard to let go of the reins of your business from time to time. It really is much better in the long run, however, to let the people you trust fail once in a while. The lessons they learn will benefit everyone going forward. It's analogous to being a parent when you know your child is about to make a really stupid fucking choice, but you let them make it anyway, because you know it will be good for them to fall flat on their face and learn from it.

Conclusion

NOW GO DO IT!

Far better it is to dare mighty things, to win glorious triumphs, even though checkered by failure, than to take rank with those poor spirits who neither enjoy much nor suffer much, because they live in the gray twilight that knows neither victory nor defeat.

—THEODORE ROOSEVELT (PROGRESSIVE THINKER, KICK-ASS TREE PLANTER, AND ESTEEMED TWENTY-SIXTH PRESIDENT OF THE UNITED STATES)

If you've read this far, you're probably ready to take that plunge and change the world with your best idea. If so, congratulations are definitely in order! The purpose of dedicating a year of my life to this book will be worth it if these eleven chapters have served you as inspiration, motivation, and even some preparation for what you're about to experience.

Now you know that your journey will include some tough times. Hopefully they won't be as extreme as getting stranded in the Saudi Arabian desert or being within a whisker of getting thrown in a Malagasy prison. However, if something like that does happen to you, I hope you'll learn as much from your experience as I did from mine. Each time you encounter such a challenging conflict, you'll have an opportunity to graduate your mindset.

The most essential tool you can call upon to rise up and move on from these situations will always be your *why*. Once you understand *why* you want to introduce your idea to the world, you will succeed. Always remember that sheer revenue does not define your ultimate success or failure. Instead, success will be determined by the extent to which you fulfill your mission; it is the degree to which you answer the question of *why* you are in business.

For WOODCHUCK, we define success by the amount of reforestation we have done for the planet and the millions of acres of pristine nature we've protected across the globe. Other companies may define success as the degree to which they've cured disease or solved world hunger. Still others may have a mission to connect humanity at a deeper level without electronic devices. Maybe for some, it's just about helping people to play better fucking badminton. No matter what your *why* is, that should be your measuring stick of success.

None of those ideas are going to happen, however, if you don't start to graduate your mindset right away and take that first step.

Remember, the world needs your fucking ideas. Now, go fucking put them into action!

Want to chat? Want more info? Reach out to me @benjaminjovandenwymelenberg.

There's no better to place to disconnect through journaling than next to penguins in Antarctica. (Yes, this journal is perfectly angled to show the beautiful woodgrain.)

ABOUT THE AUTHOR

Benjamin VandenWymelenberg went from being a broke-ass farm boy in Wisconsin to the founder and CEO of a multimillion-dollar business with a social conscience at the heart of its business model.

When he first started, he had no idea how to run a company, no Ivy League business degree for verification of his idea, and no money, but he made it work anyway. First and foremost, he took that first step and learned valuable lessons throughout his journey.

Ben survived failure several times and persevered through all of it. Each time presented with a challenge, he focused on graduating his mindset because he knew *why* he was in business. It was never exclusively about making money. He was in business to put nature back into people's lives, build quality American products, and create jobs in the US.

His corporate motto at WOODCHUCK USA is to "BUY ONE. PLANT ONE.®" It has already served as inspiration to plant millions of trees on six continents, with a positive environmental impact on all seven. Now he wants to help others start their own universe-saving ideas that exist within all of us. Knowing your *why* will get you through the tough times. But taking that first step will be the moment that allows your idea to someday change the world.

Appendix I

THE SPARKNOTES VERSION

---

1. You can make money doing almost anything in life, but by knowing your why, you could create significant positive impact for yourself and everyone around you.
2. Whether you're involved in personal, business, or financial relationships, you need to commit. You can't half-ass anything and expect positive results.
3. Opportunities could be hidden; you may need to look really fucking hard to find them. When you do, the rewards could be tremendous.
4. Rather than getting discouraged about a particularly difficult challenge in life or in business, graduate your mindset to view it as opportunity for growth.
5. At the end of the day, you need to be able to sell your idea. Otherwise, it's just an idea, not a business. You

have to figure out how somebody will be willing to pay money for your idea.
6. Ask questions fearlessly! Finding people who can consistently help you to gain valuable knowledge is the key to continued growth as an entrepreneur and a person.
7. Of course, it's totally fine if spirituality isn't a big part of your life; it's not for everybody. Just make sure your conscious circle includes everything that is important to you.
8. Many visionaries and entrepreneurs sacrifice their dreams for a significant other who doesn't see the bigger picture. Ensure your special someone supports your idea to change the world. Chances are this individual is part of your conscious circle, because they're obviously a huge part of your life. Therefore, their support is undeniably necessary.
9. Find trustworthy and loyal people to be on your team at all times.
10. Embrace whatever makes you or your business unique. For example, if you believe strongly in a dog-friendly work environment, let everybody know about it. At least that way you won't make the mistake of hiring someone who's allergic to dogs, or worse, a cat person!
11. Whether you're climbing a mountain or running a business, if you have that same high level of teamwork, success is inevitable. If everybody is pushing

toward the same end goal and willing to die for it, your true boundaries are much further than you have ever dreamed possible.

12. Especially when starting your business, you need to create some headspace, some time to disconnect and reset. Doing this, perhaps on a weekly basis, will better enable you to fully show up for your business and your employees.
13. If there's one thing that you take from this book (well, I hope there's more than one thing you take from it), make journaling an active part of your day, week, or month.
14. Many situations call for a balance between leadership and empowerment. This occurs when the situation is too demanding for any one person—even the business owner—to get the job done. When this happens, you need to get your hands dirty and work with the team.

Appendix II

REFERENCE MATERIALS

—

Chitwood, Roy. *World Class Selling*: Book Publishers Network, 1995.

Goggins, David. *Can't Hurt Me*. Read by Adam Skolnick and David Goggins. Place of publication: Lioncrest Publishing, Austin, TX, 2018. Audible Audiobook, 13 hours., 37 minutes.

Sinek, Simon. "How Great Leaders Inspire Action" TED Talk, TEDx Puget Sound, September 2009.

Wickman, Gino. *Traction*: BenBella Books, Dallas, TX, 2007.